Everything You Need To Know About British Titles And Honours

Fascinating Facts, Titles, Ranks Of the Hereditary Peerage, Life Peers And Honours System

by

Joanne Hayle

Text copyright © 2015 Joanne Hayle

Introduction

British titles and chivalric honours are fascinating.

They are steeped in history, tradition and ceremony and are a part of Britain's enviably rich heritage.

In the hereditary peerage we have dukes at the top and barons at the fifth rank down.

In the chivalric orders we have The Most Noble Order of the Garter as the premier honour through eight other orders to the Order of the Companions of Honour.

In this book I explore what these titles mean, when they were created and who by.

I discover what limits are applied to the number of people appointed to an honour at any one time and what ceremonial dress is designated to each order.

Several notable figures have declined particular honours; some might surprise you.

Also, learn about present title holders that have little of the expansive estates and wealth that their forebears enjoyed.

There are hereditary peers who have seen their rank in the peerage rise over the centuries and with it their place in social, political and economic spheres.
Today, the number of life peers far exceeds the number of hereditary peers that sit in the House of Lords, find out why this is.

The New Years honours and the Queen's Birthday honours are public reminders of the inspiring acts of citizens of Britain and the Commonwealth and many of us look with interest at the celebrities who "get the gong" or another medal of the British Empire.

Below, I've given you a quick reference guide to the ranks, honours and their post-nominal's i.e. the letters that can be placed after a recipient's name.

For example H.R.H Prince Richard, The Duke of Gloucester places KG and KCVO after his name.

This means that he is a Knight of the Garter and Knight Grand Cross of the Royal Victorian Order.

The Ranks of the Peerage In Order of Precedence

Duke

Marquess (or Marquis in Scotland)

Earl

Viscount

Baron

The Current British Orders of Chivalry and Their Post Nominal Letters

The Most Noble Order of the Garter - KG/LG

The Most Ancient and Most Noble Order of the Thistle - KT/LT

The Most Honourable Order of the Bath - GCB/KCB or DCB/GB

The Most Distinguished Order of St. Michael and St. George - GCMG/KCMG or DCMG/CMG*

The Royal Victorian Order - GCVO/KCVO or

DCVO/CVO/LVO/MVO

The Order of Merit - OM

The Imperial Service Order - ISO

The Most Excellent Order of the British Empire -

GBE/KBE/DBE/CBE/MBE/OBE

The Order of the Companions of Honour - CH

*The Distinguished Service Order is a wartime military honour positioned before The Royal Victorian Order. Military awards will be discussed in another book

Part One - The Peerage

Dukes

Marquesses

Earls

Viscounts

Barons

More Extinct Titles

Life Peers

Chapter 1 - Dukes

Dukes are the highest ranking hereditary peers ahead of marquesses, earls, viscounts and barons, in that order.

Origins and History

The title of Duke originated from the Latin word *dux* which means leader of a province.

It was a term used in Roman times to refer to a military commander without a precise rank.

The holder of the title also had a sovereign status, for instance, William the Conqueror was also the Duke of Normandy.

In 1337 King Edward III created the title of Duke of Cornwall for his eldest son.

This tradition is still honoured in the present day. H.R.H. Prince Charles, Prince of Wales is the Duke of Cornwall and the Duke of Rothesay (A Scottish title.)

Richard II was the second holder of the dukedom of Cornwall; he was the grandson of Edward III. His father Edward, The Black Prince died before his accession.

Edward III also created the dukedoms of Clarence and Lancaster for two of his sons.
John of Gaunt was the 1st Duke of Lancaster and Lionel of Antwerp was the 1st Duke of Clarence.

There had been a previous Duke of Lancaster, Henry of Grosmont, from 1351 to 1361 The title was recreated for John of Gaunt.

Richard II made his remaining uncles dukes. Edmund of Langley was created the 1st Duke of York and Thomas of Woodstock was the 1st Duke of Gloucester.

The first non royal dukedom was created in 1448 for the man who had previously been titled Sir William de la Pole and the Marquess of Suffolk. In 1448 he became the Duke of Suffolk.

By the time that the Tudor era began although thirty one dukedoms had been created only two, those of Lancaster and Cornwall were still in use.

John Howard had inherited the Dukedom of Norfolk in 1483 through his mother, Margaret Mowbray's, blood line. Her father had received the title of Duke in 1397.

The Norfolk line died out at the Battle of Bosworth Field when the Duke of Norfolk had fought and died with Richard III. Henry VIII resurrected the title on 1st February 1514 for Thomas Howard, the great grandfather of Queen Elizabeth I and the grandfather of Anne Boleyn and Katherine Howard.

There were no dukes by the end of Elizabeth I's reign. The fourth Duke of Norfolk had been executed for treason and the Dukedoms of Lancaster and Cornwall were dormant, Elizabeth bore no children.

The Stuart monarchs resurrected or restored some of the extinct titles.

Once again there were Duke's of Norfolk.

At that time Parliament conferred dukedoms.

A ceremonial sword was fastened to a cincture, a belt based and used in religion; this meant that you had been appointed a duke.

This ceremony was abandoned in 1615 and a letters patent under the Great Seal, the sovereign's seal, was created for the purpose.

The most recently created dukedom is Westminster. It was created in 1874 during Queen Victoria's reign for Hugh Grosvenor, 3rd Marquess of Westminster.

The premier non royal duke is the Duke of Norfolk.

In Scotland this honour rests with the Duke's of Hamilton and Brandon, this title was created in 1643.

In Ireland the Duke of Leinster is the premier duke. This title was created in 1766.

The Current Royal Dukedoms

Queen Elizabeth II holds the titles of the Duke of Lancaster and the Duke of Normandy. Lancaster belongs to the crown. Queen Victoria decided that "Duke" was the correct title for the owner of a dukedom whether they were male or female. This means that the Queen is the Duke rather than the Duchess of Lancaster and people in the county of Lancaster may raise a toast to "The Queen, Duke of Lancaster."

The Duchy of Normandy, held by the English monarchs since William the Conqueror, included the Channel Islands. In 1204 King Philip II Augustus of France had seized the mainland Normandy territories from King John. Since 1259 the Channel Islands have been self governing and they are not part of the United Kingdom but they swear allegiance to the monarch, currently Queen Elizabeth II, the Duke of Normandy. They are termed Crown Dependencies.

There are seven current royal dukedoms:

1st Duke of Cambridge - Prince William

1st Duke of Edinburgh - Prince Philip

2nd Duke of Gloucester - Prince Richard

2nd Duke of Kent - Prince George

1st Duke of York - Prince Andrew

Duke of Cornwall and Duke of Rothesay - Prince Charles.

Cornwall and Rothesay are not hereditary titles but they are traditionally bestowed on the monarch's eldest son either from their birth or on the monarch's accession. There is no numerical addition to these titles.

There is nothing about a dukedom that makes it royal except that it is held by a member of the royal family.
In 1520 a decree by the Lord Chamberlain stated that a "Duke of the Blood Royal" was to receive precedence over a peer not related to the sovereign but this does not extend to all royal

descendants.

When H.R.H Prince Philip, Duke of Edinburgh dies his title will revert to the crown and it has been announced that H.R.H Prince Edward, Earl of Wessex will be given the title.

However, Edward's descendants will hold it as a non royal dukedom.

James, currently Viscount Severn, will be the first of these descendants.

When the current Dukes of Gloucester and Kent die their titles will go to the present Earls of Ulster and St. Andrews but the dukedoms will not be royal.

The earls are not H.R.H, unlike their fathers who were the sons of George V.

Sons of the monarch usually become dukes at the time of their marriage.

If she wishes to the Queen can, as she did with Prince William, bestow royal dukedoms on her grandchildren.

William was the most recent recipient of this honour. In 2011 he was created the 1st Duke of Cambridge.

In 1986 when Prince Andrew married Sarah Ferguson he was given the title of Duke of York.

The Current Non Royal British Dukedoms

The order of precedence is as follows:

Dukes created by an English monarch.

Dukes created by a King of Scotland.

Dukes of Great Britain with titles created 1707 – 1801.

Dukes of Ireland (in 1801 the United Kingdom peerage

included Ireland.)

Dukes of the United Kingdom.

The year of the creation of the title can also be used to

determine the order of precedence.

The Dukedoms of Monmouth, Southampton, St. Albans,

Grafton, Richmond and Lennox were created by King Charles

II for his illegitimate sons.

The Monmouth and Southampton lines are extinct.

Charles' favourite mistresses were also given titles, the

Duchess of Cleveland for Barbara Castlemaine and the Duchess of Portsmouth for Louise de Penancoët de Kérouaille.

The Current Dukes In Alphabetical Order:

James Hamilton is the 5th Duke of Abercorn.

1979-present.

The title was created in 1868 in Ireland.

Torquhil Ian Campbell is the 13th Duke of Argyll.

2001-present.

The Scottish title was created in 1701.

The United Kingdom's Duke of Argyll title was created in 1892 and is currently held by its 6th recipient, the above 13th Duke of Argyll in the Scottish peerage.

John Murray is the 11th Duke of Atholl.

1996-present.

It is a Scottish title created in 1703.

David Robert Somerset is the 11th Duke of Beaufort.

1984-present.

This English title originated in 1682.

Andrew Ian Henry Russell is the 15th Duke of Bedford.

2003-present.

Created in 1663, it is an English title.

Angus Alan Douglas Douglas Hamilton is the 12th Duke of Brandon and 15th Duke of Hamilton.

1973-present.

The Scottish title of Duke of Hamilton was created in 1643, the Duke of Brandon title was created in 1711 of Great Britain.

Walter Francis John Montagu-Scott is the 9th Duke of Buccleuch.

1973-present.

This is a Scottish title dating back to 1663 and he also holds the Scottish title of 11th Duke of Queensbury, created in 1684.

Peregrine Andrew Morny Cavendish is the 12th Duke of Devonshire.

2004-present.

This is an English title from 1694.

James George Alexander Bannerman Carnegie is the 3rd Duke of Fife.

1959-present.

This is a title of the United Kingdom, conferred since 1900.

Hugh Denis Charles Fitzroy is the 11th Duke of Grafton.

1970-present.

Issued in 1675, it is an English title.

Maurice Fitzgerald is the 9th Duke of Leinster.

2004-present.

Dating back to 1766, it is the premier Irish title.

Alexander Charles David Drogo Montagu is the 13th Duke of Manchester.

2002-present.

It is a title of Great Britain created in 1719.

Charles James Spencer-Churchill is the 12th Duke of Marlborough.

October 2014-present.

This is an English title dating back to 1702.

James Graham is the 8th Duke of Montrose.

1992-present.

This is a Scottish title from 1707.

Edward William Fitzalan-Howard is the 18th Duke of Norfolk.

2002-present.

Duke of Norfolk has been an English title since 1483 - see above.

Ralph George Algernon Percy is the 12th Duke of Northumberland.

1995-present.

Created as a title of Great Britain in 1766.

Charles Henry Gordon-Lennox is the 10th Duke of Richmond. 1989-present.
Created in 1675, the Duke of Richmond is also the Scottish 10th Duke of Lennox, and the 5th Duke of Gordon in the United Kingdom.

Guy David Innes-Ker is the 10th Duke of Roxburghe. 1974-present.
Duke of Roxburghe is a Scottish title created in 1707.

David Charles Robert Manners is the 11thDuke of Rutland. 1999 to present.
Created 1703, it is an English title.

.

Murray de Vere Beauclerk is the 14th Duke of St. Albans. 1988-present.
This is an English title created in 1684.

John Michael Edward Seymour is the 19th Duke of Somerset.

1984-present.

This is an English title from 1547.

Francis Ronald Egerton is the 7th Duke of Sutherland

2000-present.

This is a title of the United Kingdom created in 1833.

Arthur Valerian Wellesley is the 8th Duke of Wellington.

1972-present.

Another United Kingdom title, created in 1814.

Gerald Cavendish Grosvenor is the 6th Duke of Westminster.

1979-present.

The most recently created title of the United Kingdom, 1874.

The Titles Of These Dukes Heirs

Duke of Abercorn

Heir: The Marquess of Hamilton.

Duke of Argyll

Heir: The Marquess of Kintyre and Lorne.

Duke of Atholl

Heir: The Marquess of Tullibardine

Duke of Beaufort

Heir: The Marquess of Worcester.

Duke of Bedford

Heir: The Marquess of Tavistock.

Duke of Brandon and Duke of Hamilton

Heir: The Marquess of Douglas and Clydesdale.

Duke of Buccleuch and Duke of Queensbury

Heir: The Earl of Dalkeith.

Duke of Devonshire

Heir: The Marquess of Hartington.

Duke of Fife

Heir: The Earl of Southesk.

Duke of Grafton

Heir: The Earl of Euston.

Duke of Leinster

Heir: Captain Lord John Fitzgerald.

Duke of Manchester

Heir: Viscount Mandeville.

Duke of Marlborough

Heir: The Marquess of Blandford

Duke of Montrose

Heir: The Marquess of Graham.

Duke of Norfolk

Heir: The Earl of Arundel and Surrey.

Duke of Northumberland

Heir: Earl Percy.

Duke of Richmond,Duke of Lennox, 5th Duke of Gordon

Heir: The Earl of March and Kinrara.

Duke of Roxburghe

Heir: The Marquess of Bowmont and Cessford.

Duke of Rutland

Heir: The Marquess of Granby.

Duke of St. Albans

Heir: The Earl of Burford.

Duke of Somerset

Heir: Lord Seymour.

Duke of Sutherland

Heir: The Marquess of Stafford.

Duke of Wellington

Heir: The Marquess of Douro.

Duke of Westminster

Heir: Earl Grosvenor.

Forms of Address

Duke's are referred to as Your Grace or His Grace.

A Duchess is either Your Grace or Her Grace.

A Duke's eldest son normally takes one of his father's subsidiary titles.

The Duke of Norfolk's heir is the Earl of Arundel and Surrey, the earldom is one of the several honours that the Duke holds.

Younger sons and daughters are referred to as Lord or Lady. Examples of this are the 9th Duke of Wellington's younger children, Lord Frederick Wellesley, Lady Mary and Lady Charlotte Wellesley. Their elder brother Arthur, Marquess of Douro is the heir to the dukedom.

The Coronet

The non royal coronet, a small crown with ornamentation on a metal rim, for a duke has eight strawberry leaves.

This can be worn at coronations and on coats of arms.

Royal duke's coronets have four crosses and four strawberry leaves alternating.

Spotlight

The Duke's of Norfolk can trace their lineage back to King's Edward I and Edward III.

The current Duke holds the family's extensive land and properties

Arundel Castle in West Sussex is the ancestral home of the Dukes of Norfolk.

The castle is a Grade I listed building and it has been in the family's possession since the eleventh century.

Carlton Towers in Yorkshire is a Grade I listed house. Lord Gerald Fitzalan-Howard, the Duke's younger brother resides there.

It is often used for location filming in dramas.

Clun Castle in Shropshire is owned by the Duke but English Heritage maintain its ruins.

The Duke of Norfolk owns land in London which is estimated to be worth over £100 million.

The Norfolk's once owned Worksop Manor in Nottinghamshire, Framlingham Castle and Bungay Castle in Suffolk and Norfolk House in London.

General Eisenhower used Norfolk House as a base during the Second World War.

It is now offices.

The Dukes had land in Glossop, Derbyshire, they sold it in 1925.

The 9th Duke of Leinster, the premier Duke of Ireland lives in a farmhouse in Oxfordshire, England and he works as a landscape designer.

The family's wealth decreased over the centuries thanks to ill fated business ventures and gambling.

The ancestral home was Carton House located to the west of Dublin, Ireland.

It was sold by the 7th Duke of Leinster to cover gambling debts. Unfortunately, the 7th Duke was later declared bankrupt.

Carton House is open today as a golfing hotel.

Past Dukes also owned Leinster House.

The property was sold by the 3rd Duke in 1815 to the Royal

Dublin Society.

The society sold it to the Irish Dail (parliament) in 1924, the

Dail has been housed there since 1922.

The present Duke of Hamilton and Brandon has large quarters

in Holyrood Palace, the official home of Queen Elizabeth II

when she is in Scotland.

He is the Hereditary Keeper of Holyrood Palace.

The Duke is a unique figure; he is the only person who may

take the crown jewels out of the city of Edinburgh.

He is the Hereditary Bearer of the Crown of Scotland.

The ancestral home lies outside of Edinburgh at Lennoxlove.

The Dukes owned Hamilton Palace in South Lanarkshire,

Scotland, sadly it was demolished in the 1920's after it had

fallen into disrepair.

The Hamilton Mausoleum is open to the public.

Chatelherault Hunting Lodge was owned by the family between 1732 and 1973. It was given to the state in lieu of death duties.
The property has been renovated and it too is open to the public.

Cadzow Castle was built in the thirteenth century and given to the Hamilton's by Robert the Bruce.
The ruins of the keep remain and excavation work continues there.

Over the centuries many other properties have been in the ownership of these Dukes. Some stand as ruins in South Lanarkshire, Renfrewshire and East Lothian.

Notable Refusals

Sir Winston Churchill, the former Prime Minister, was offered the Dukedom of London. He declined so that he could still sit in the House of Commons and it also allowed his son Randolph to pursue a political career which as a peer he could not have done.

Benjamin Disraeli, 1st Earl of Beaconsfield, a favourite of Queen Victoria and a Prime Minister declined a dukedom although he had previously accepted an earldom.

When Prince Louis of Battenburg, the former First Sea Lord of the British Navy who had married Queen Victoria's granddaughter, Princess Victoria of Hesse and by Rhine, renounced their German titles in 1917 King George V offered him a dukedom.
Louis opted for a marquessate instead because he could not afford the extravagant costs involved with the lifestyle of a duke.

Therefore, he was created the Marquess of Milford Haven.

Chapter 2 – Marquesses

Marquess is a lesser rank than a duke and a higher rank than an earl.

The Scottish spelling is often marquis rather than marquess.

Origins and History

The Normans called earls or barons tasked with guarding the Welsh and Scottish Borders as *Marchio*.

The French word *Marchis* which meant ruler of a border area from the word *marche* (frontier) entered the English language in the 14th century.

It was believed that their land was harder to defend against attack because it was in the Marches or border areas. However, the exact reason for the resulting distinction in the titles marquess and earl is unclear.

The 9th Earl of Oxford, Robert de Vere was the first English

Marquess.

He was created the Marquess of Dublin by Richard II in 1385 by the issue of a letters patent under the Great Seal. He was not Marquess for long; in October 1386 he was created the Duke of Ireland.

The first Earl of Somerset was an illegitimate son of John of Gaunt, the first Duke of Lancaster.

In 1397 he became the Marquess of Dorset. The title was revoked two years later when the Marquess fell in to disgrace.

The title of Marquess was dormant until 1442 when Henry VI revived it.

Henry VIII conferred the title of Marquess of Pembroke on Anne Boleyn prior to their marriage and she is the only woman in history to have been a marquess in her own right.

The ceremonial duties were carried out on 1st September 1532 at Windsor Castle.

The number of marquesses created was not vast.

Apparently when Queen Victoria asked her first Prime Minister Lord Melbourne why this was he replied that it was not an *English* title and that it was felt that a marquessate was given when the monarch did not wish to bestow a dukedom on the person concerned.

It's unknown whether these observations were a broadly adopted view or if they were his opinion.

Royal Marquesses

There have been no new royal marquesses for almost a hundred years.

In 1917 George V's German relatives renounced their titles in favour of British ones, for instance Prince Adolphus of Teck, Queen Mary's brother, became the Marquess of Cambridge. His son, George, the second marquess died in 1981.
He had one child, a daughter, Lady Mary, she died in 1999.
The name of Cambridge was resurrected as a dukedom for Prince William.

The first Marquess and Marchioness of Milford Haven were the former Prince and Princess Louis of Battenburg.
George Mountbatten is the fourth Marquess of Milford Haven.
He owns the 1100 acre Great Trippetts Estate in Milland, Sussex.

Lyndon Manor in Holyport, Berkshire was lived in by the

second Marquess between 1928 and 1933.

Moyns Park in Essex, a grade I listed property, was left to the fourth Marquess and his younger brother Ivar by Josephine Hartford Bryce.

The third Marquess had been married to Janet Mercedes Bryce, a niece of Mrs Hartford Bryce's by marriage and the mother of the current Marquess and his brother.

A Dukedom has not been conferred on the family since his ancestor's refusal in 1917.

The cost of being a Duke would not be a factor anymore (see chapter 1 Notable Refusals) *if* the news reports of 2006 were correct, the 4th Marquess sold his company uSwitch for £210 million. ($400million.)

Non Royal Marquesses

The creation of marquesses appears to have been halted after 1936 when Freeman Freeman-Thomas, formerly Baron Willingon, Viscount Willingdon and Viscount Ratendone become a marquess.

The second marquess took the title on his father's death in 1941.

Inigo Brassey Freeman-Thomas married three times but had no issue.

When he died on 19th March 1979 the marquessate became extinct.

The courtesy title of Marquess is often used by the heir to a dukedom. The heir needs to be a rank below the Duke so in the hierarchy of titles, Marquess is one below and therefore appropriate.

Nigel Paulet, the 18th Marquess of Winchester is the sole Marquess in the Peerage of England and therefore he is the most senior by default.

There are:

Four Marquesses of Scotland.

Six Marquesses of Great Britain.

Eight Irish Marquesses.

Fifteen Marquesses of the United Kingdom.

There are no Marchionesses in their own right.

This makes a grand total of thirty four.

The current Marquess of Winchester lives in South Africa. The title was created in 1551 for William Paulet, 1st Earl of Wiltshire. He had been created Baron St. John in 1539 and Earl of Wiltshire in 1550.

He was the Lord High Treasurer between 1550 and 1572 during the reigns of Edward VI, Mary I and Elizabeth I, possibly because he did not mind changing religions to please the monarch.

The sixth Marquess was created the Duke of Bolton but the dukedom became extinct on Christmas Day 1794 when Admiral Harry Powlett (Paulet) died.

The marquessate passed to his cousin George Paulet.

The current marquess inherited the title from his cousin Richard Paulet in 1968, he'd died unmarried and without an heir.

The Marquesses of Winchester are the only marquesses not to have a dukedom in their possession.

The premier Marquess of Scotland is Granville Gordon, the 13th Marquess of Huntly.

The 6th Earl of Huntly, George Gordon, was created the 1st Marquess of Huntly on 7th April 1599.

The family's home is at Aboyne Castle, a thirteenth century castle in Aberdeenshire, Scotland.

It was restored by the current Marquess of Huntly in the late 1970's.

As the leaders of Clan Gordon the Marquesses owned Huntly Castle in Huntly, Aberdeenshire.

It was sold in 1923 and the ruins are maintained by Historic Scotland.

Through Lord Frederick Gordon, a son of the 9th Marquess of Huntly the family became close to the throne.

He married Lady Augusta Fitzclarence, one of King William IV's illegitimate daughters by the actress Dorothy Jordan.

Augusta became Lady Augusta Gordon on 24th August 1836, it was her second marriage, her first husband had died in 1831.

They had no surviving children.

In 1837 she was appointed as the State Housekeeper to Kensington Palace.

Lord Frederick was a sailor but he was also a Lord of the Bedchamber to his father in law from October 1836.

He was made an Admiral in 8th April 1868.

Augusta died in 1865.

When Lord Frederick inherited his uncle's estate in 1843, he added the surname Hallyburton to the end of the name in his honour.

The premier Marquess of Ireland is the Marquess of Waterford.

The marquessate was created in 1789 for George de la Poer Beresford, the 2nd Earl of Tyrone.

The family seat is at Curraghmore in County Waterford, south east Ireland.

The eighth Marquess John Hubert de la Poer Beresford died on 11th February 2015 aged eighty one and his son Henry became the ninth Marquess of Waterford.

The heir to the marquessate is Richard John de la Poer Beresford, currently a professional polo player using the name Richard Le Poer.

Forms Of Address

They are formally addressed as The Most Honourable The Marquess of e.g. Exeter/Hertford/Anglesey.
The female form is The Most Honourable The Marchioness...

Informally they are referred to as Lord or My Lord. The female forms are Lady or My Lady.

The heir to the marquessate usually takes a courtesy title of their father's.
The 10th Marquess of Londonderry has Earl Vane and Viscount Castlereagh to issue to his heir in the future should he have any children.
He was known as Viscount Castlereagh before he became the 10th Marquess.
Currently his heir is his brother, Lord Reginald-Vane–Tempest-Stewart.

A marquess by courtesy title is not given the mantle of The

Most Honourable they are called Marquess (of) e.g. Douro. This marquess will become His Grace The Duke of Wellington after his father dies.

The Duke of Westminster also holds the titles Earl Grosvenor and Marquess of Westminster. His son uses the courtesy title of Earl Grosvenor so there is a lack of confusion but if he and the Duke had wished he could have used Marquess of Westminster.

Younger children of marquesses are titled Lord and Lady. So, using Westminster as an example again, the other children were Lady Tamara, Lady Edwina and Lady Viola Grosvenor. Lady Tamara and Lady Edwina are now married with children.

Incidentally, Earl Grosvenor is one of Prince George of Cambridge's godparents, the late Princess Diana, Princess of Wales was Edwina's godmother.

Coronet

The coronet for a marquess has four strawberry leaves, three of which are visible, alternating with four silver pearls, of which two are visible.

Marquesses may use the coronet on a coat of arms and on ceremonial occasions.

Spotlight

Robert Michael James Gascoyne-Cecil, the 7th Marquess of Salisbury enjoyed a political career as Viscount Cranborne (his father was the 6th Marquess) and he was also a Leader of the House of Lords.

He was given a life peerage in 1999 and was titled Baron Gascoyne-Cecil of Essendon in the County of Rutland.

He became 7th Marquess in 2003.

The family seat is at Hatfield House, a country house set in vast parkland.

It was once a home to Queen Elizabeth I and it was given to the family by King James I in exchange for their property Theobolds.

Hatfield House is open to the public.

The family own land in London, Dorset and Hertfordshire and a number of Hatfield heirlooms.

The Sunday Times Rich List noted that the marquess' wealth sat at over £250 million in 2008.

Frederick William Augustus Hervey is The 8th Marquess of Bristol.
The marquessate was created for the 5th Earl of Bristol in 1826.

Ickworth House on the Ickworth Estate in Suffolk was the family seat from the fifteenth century until 1998.

The Hervey's traditional burial place is Ickworth Church.

When the fourth Marquess died in 1956 his widow gave the house and grounds to the National Trust in lieu of death duties. She stipulated at that time that a home should always be made available to the Marquesses of Bristol at Ickworth.

The National Trust gave a ninety nine year lease to the

following Marquesses of Bristol so that they could reside in the East Wing of the house on the condition that they paid yearly expenses to the Trust.

In 1998 the 7th Marquess sold the remainder of his lease to the National Trust, it has been suggested that this was because he was facing eviction due his behaviour as a tenant.
He died in 1998 and the current Marquess has spoken out about not being given the opportunity to repurchase the East Wing in his ancestral home.

The National Trust converted the East Wing in to a hotel.

The current Marquess is involved in businesses and his sisters Lady Victoria and Lady Isabella have both achieved reality television fame.

The family fortune diminished under Victor, the 6th Marquess, their father.
He appears to have been an interesting figure, he was a

playboy nicknamed The Reptile, he was also a convicted jewel thief and a bankrupt. He married three times.

The 7th Marquess, the 8th Marquess' older half brother followed his father's lead.

He is rumoured to have spent over £21 or £31 million, depending on which source you refer to.

He died at the age of forty four and another half brother committed suicide.

The 8th Marquess has no issue so his heir is his fourth cousin, once removed, Alexander Hervey.

Notable Refusals

Henry Lascalles, the fifth Earl Harewood refused a marquessate in 1922, interestingly because he believed that they died out more quickly than earldoms.

His son, Viscount Lascelles, later the sixth Marquess, was married to Princess Mary, Princess Royal, the daughter of George V and Queen Mary from 28th February 1922.

John Poyntz Spencer, fifth Earl Spencer, nicknamed Red Earl because of his flaming red beard, declined a marquessate despite having been a groom to Prince Albert and the Prince of Wales, later King Edward VII, a close friend of Prime Minister William Gladstone, he served during all of Gladstone's terms in office, he was the Lord Lieutenant of Ireland twice and the First Lord of the Admiralty and considered for the Prime Minister's role twice.

He did accept the Order of the Garter.

Although he married, he was childless and so he was succeeded by his half brother, Charles Spencer.

Chapter 3 – Earls

Origins and History

Originally, in the rank below *dux*, the dukes, were the *duces* (the plural of dux.)

The Anglo Saxon name for duces was the *ealdormanry*. This title was replaced by the Danish version *eorl* and this spelling changed to earl as time passed.

Earls in England held the equivalent rank of European Counts. Earls served the monarch by conducting the administration of their designated area and collecting taxes and fines from the citizens under their jurisdiction.
For this, they received a third of the money that they gathered.

In Edward the Confessor's reign (1043-1066) the areas that the earls controlled were more like small kingdoms.
William the Conqueror changed this when he came to the

throne, he divided England in to shires and these shires became counties.

During Norman times new earldoms were created but there was a significant difference between the new ones and the existing earls, the new earls were not deployed as tax collectors or placed in charge of legal matters.

The Earl of Cheshire and the Earl of Shropshire were among this new group.

Earldoms were not great in number.

King Stephen, William's grandson reigned 1135-1154.

He keenly rewarded his allies with earldoms, property and the power to overrule local sheriffs.

Unfortunately, some earls decided that this permitted them to create their own courts and currencies. This was not what the King had intended or envisaged.

Henry II took control of the castles that Stephen had awarded in his reign and had some of the properties that the unruly earls had built without the King's approval razed to the ground.

The earls were placed under the King's strict control and he created no new earls.

Earldoms were either inherited or married in to and the monarch could, if he wished to, decide that the title of Earl could not be transferred to the bridegroom.

The sheriffs benefitted from this curtailment of the earls' power by receiving more authority except in rural or distant counties like Cornwall or in the Welsh Marches.

Before dukes, earls were considered to be the rank below princes of the realm but by the thirteenth century they had no more power than any other nobleman.

In the 14th century the creation of an earl was marked by a ceremony similar to that of a duke's investiture. The King tied a sword belt around the waist of the new earl which told observers that the monarch had empowered him.

The earls were perceived as close friends and favourites of the King but this was not always so in reality, the earls around King Edward II deposed him in January 1327 in favour of his son, Edward III, and the unwanted King was murdered at Berkeley Castle.

Edward II's wife Isabella of France and her lover Roger Mortimor had led the rebellion.

Mortimor was the third Baron Mortimor at the time but he was created 1st Earl of March in September 1328.

Edward III had him hanged in 1330.

Mortimor had not been popular with the existing earls and they were keen to diminish his power.

In Scotland the oldest earldoms were taken from the title Mormaer of a particular location and these Mormaer's morphed in to earldoms. The Mormaer of Fife was often the nobleman who crowned the new King of Scotland.

The title of earl was normally associated with a place, for example, the Earl of Derby and the Earl of Warwick but there are earldoms that don't belong to a location, these include Earl Spencer, Earl Grey and Earl Cadogan.

Former Prime Ministers were normally offered an earldom when they retired from office. This tradition ceased with Harold Macmillan in 1984. He was created Earl of Stockton.

Royal Earls

H.R.H. Prince Edward was created the Earl of Wessex and

Viscount Severn when he married Sophie Rhys-Jones on 19th

June 1999. Sophie is H.R.H. the Countess of Wessex.

It was determined at the time of their marriage that their

children would be styled as the children of an earl not as the

children of a prince.

Their son James is known by the title of Viscount Severn.

Their daughter is Lady Louise Windsor.

George Windsor, the Earl of St. Andrews is the eldest son of

the H.R.H. Edward, Duke of Kent. The earldom is one of his

fathers and George uses it as a courtesy title.

When he inherits the title of Duke it will not be a royal

dukedom as it is at the present time.

The Earl of St. Andrews married a divorcee and relinquished

his place in the line of succession. This does not stop him

inheriting the dukedom.

He has worked as a diplomat and is a patron of several

charities.

His son, Edward, Lord Downpatrick will be the first Roman Catholic Duke of Kent since the reformation.

Alexander Windsor, the son of H.R.H. Prince Richard, Duke of Gloucester is known as the Earl of Ulster, one of his father's subsidiary titles, or more normally as Alex Ulster.

Alexander served in the military for several years and is involved in charity work.

His wife, the Countess of Ulster is known professionally as Dr. Claire Booth.

Their son, Xan, Baron Culloden will become the Earl of Ulster when his father inherits the dukedom and Lady is the courtesy title of their daughter Cosima.

Alexander and his descendants will not hold the title as a royal dukedom.

Antony Armstrong-Jones was the husband of the Queen's late

sister, Margaret Rose from 1960 until their divorce in 1978.

He was created the first Earl of Snowdon and Viscount Linley.

His son David is known as Viscount Linley, he will inherit the earldom upon his father's death.

The Earl of Snowdon is a noted photographer and he has made official portraits of the great and the good in British society and provided images for several publications.

He also designed the aviary at London Zoo, an electric wheelchair and the investiture ceremony for Prince Charles to be appointed the Prince of Wales at Caernarvon Castle in 1969.

He holds the life peerage of Baron Armstrong-Jones of Nymans in the County of Sussex so that he can sit in the House of Lords.

Non Royal Earls

There are

Twenty Earls of England.

Thirty nine Earls of Scotland.

Twenty four Earls of Great Britain.

Thirty nine Earls of Ireland.

Sixty nine Earls of the United Kingdom.

Four countesses in their own right.

This makes a grand total of one hundred and ninety five.

The premier Earl of England and Ireland is Charles Henry John Benedict Crofton Chetwynd Chetwynd-Talbot, 22nd Earl of Shrewsbury,7th Earl Talbot, 22nd Earl of Waterford and the Lord High Steward of Ireland.

The current premier Earl of Scotland is Robert Lindsay, 29th Earl of Crawford, 12th Earl of Balcarres. He is the hereditary Clan Chief of Clan Lindsay.

The 18th Duke of Norfolk as the premier Duke of England is also known as the premier Earl as he holds the title of Earl of Arundel (currently being used by his son) and he is the Earl Marshal and Hereditary Marshal of England too.

Some earls are not closely linked to the place that their title suggests.

Aubrey De Vere , the first Earl of Oxford's property lay in Essex, his seat was at Castle Hedingham near the ancient road between Colchester and Cambridge but there was already an Earl of Essex, namely Geoffrey de Mandeville II, Aubrey's brother in law, so an alternative, albeit misleading, name was taken.

The earldom was created in 1141 and it became extinct in 1703, the De Vere family had held its title for the longest time compared to other earldoms.

Robert De Vere, the third Earl of Oxford had been one of the twenty five guarantors of the Magna Carta of 1215. The last earl, another Aubrey, had fought with King Charles I as a Royalist during the English Civil War.

Forms of Address

It is absolutely incorrect to address a Countess as Countess, except in the case of H.R.H Sophie, Countess of Wessex. She is always Countess.

An Earl is referred to as Lord and so the Countess is Lady and a Countess in her own right is also termed Lady.

Earldoms can be inherited by the female line and the title of The Countess can be used by the lady although her husband, unless he is already titled, would remain a Mister.

The Earl's eldest son may use a courtesy title and the younger sons are The Honourable and the daughters are Lady.
For example Charles Spencer, the 9th Earl Spencer's eldest son Louis is Viscount Althorp, his sisters are Lady Kitty Spencer, Lady Eliza Spencer and Lady Amelia Spencer.

The exception to this rule is in Scotland when there are no

courtesy titles.

The eldest child can be styled as Master or Mistress of...

e.g. Susan, The Mistress of Mar and Kellie will be the future

Countess of Mar and Kellie.

Younger sons can be referred to as Younger of...

Coronet

An earl uses a coronet with eight strawberry leaves, with four

visible and eight pearls, with five showing.

Their rank may be shown on a coat of arms including the

coronet shown above its shield.

Spotlight

Charles Cadogan, 8th Earl of Cadogan belongs to one of the richest families in Britain.

His company Cadogan Estates Limited owns the majority of properties in the Chelsea and Knightsbridge areas of London. The current Viscount Chelsea, the Earl's son and heir, took over the day to day running of the company in 2012.

Exclusive addresses and roads lie in these areas, among them are Sloane Street, Sloane Square, Cadogan Place, Cadogan Square and Hans Place.

Sloane Street is the home of elite shops like Gucci, Roberto Cavalli, Louis Vuitton and Cartier.

At the time of writing a two bedroom apartment in Cadogan Gardens was being advertised for sale at over £3.25 million.

Since spring 2011 the company has owned the Cadogan Hotel on Sloane Street. It's believed that it was purchased for £15.4 million.

Cadogan's land is close to the Duke of Westminster's land in

Mayfair and Belgravia.

The manor of Chelsea was bought by Sir Hans Sloane in 1712 and Beaufort House, Cheyne Walk, Chelsea followed in 1737. William, Lord Cheyne had owned the manor of Chelsea before Sloane.

One of Sir Han's daughters, Elizabeth, married Charles, 2nd Baron Cadogan in 1717.

Hans Town, created from 1777, was used as a model for developers in other areas of London.

Sir Hans Sloane's manor was demolished in 1760.

By 1821 all of the land that Sir Hans Sloane had owned was in the Cadogan's ownership.

David Brudenell-Bruce, The Earl of Cardigan, is the heir to the Marquess of Ailesbury.

He is the thirty first Hereditary Warden of Savernake Forest.

The Savernake Estate has over four thousand five hundred acres of land.

In recent years a business venture turned sour, the Earl sold the lease for his ancestral home Tottenham House to an American hotel chain that subsequently went in to liquidation.

He has been in dispute with the Trustees of the Savernake Estate in recent years over proposed sales of family possessions and artwork.

In 2013 he appeared in stories in the British press stating that he was claiming £71 per week Jobseekers Allowance from the government because he was not being allowed access to his money by the trustees and that he was seeking further employment as a chauffeur or driver.

A legal dispute with the trustees found in the Earl's favour in 2014.

It was also reported in the press in 2013 that the Earl was estranged from the children from his previous marriage.

If this was or is true, one of these is Viscount Savernake, his heir.

Notable Refusals

Arthur Balfour, the former Prime Minister declined an earldom in 1919 but he had a change of heart and accepted the Earldom of Balfour in 1922.

Although Harold Macmillan, the former Prime Minister took the title Earl of Stockton in 1984 he had refused an earldom in 1963.

Sir Angus Ogilvy refused an earldom when he married H.R.H Princess Alexandra of Kent in 1963.
He also declined a grace and favour home preferring to lease a property from the Crown Estates.
He was the second son of the twelfth Earl of Airlie and so he already had the title of The Honourable.
He accepted the honour of Knight Commander of the Royal Victorian Order in 1988.
Sadly, he passed away in 2004.
His elder brother David is the thirteenth Earl of Airlie.

Chapter 4 – Viscounts

Viscounts are ranked beneath dukes, marquesses and earls but higher than barons.

Origins and History

The title is believed to have been derived from the Anglo Saxon term *shire reeve* which became contracted to the word *sheriff,* a person ordered by the King to keep the peace in a particular area.

These were not hereditary titles.

The title originated as a hereditary position in the Holy Roman Empire.

Viscounts were not created or recorded in English history until 1440, thirteen years before the end of the Hundred Years' War between England and France.

King Henry VI married Margaret of Anjou in 1445, he desired

peace rather than war, unlike some of his noblemen, and he

attempted to consolidate the titles of both countries

satisfactorily.

Lord John Beaumont was the first man to receive a dual

viscountcy, he was named Viscount Beaumont in both

England and France.

As with the other ranks of the peerage it was issued by a letters

patent under the Great Seal.

Viscountcies were not that popular, in the early period of her

reign Queen Victoria asked Lord Melbourne, her first Prime

Minister why this was. He offered her the same reason as he

had for marquesses. Viscounts were not *English*. He told her

that viscount came from the French *Vice Comites*.

Irish Viscounts were not originally entitled to sit in London's

House of Lords only the House of Commons.

It has become more common to bestow a life peerage on former Speakers of the House of Commons but between 1801 and 1983 the majority (eleven) of the retiring Speakers received viscountcies.

In London, sheriff is one of the officers of the City of London Corporation, the governing council of the centre of London. The Lord Mayor has two elected sheriffs appointed at midsummer.

These sheriffs are not viscounts.

Fiona Adler and Alderman Doctor Andrew Parmley were elected as sheriffs in June 2014.

Royal Viscounts

Viscount Linley is the son of the late H.R.H. Princess Margaret, the Queen's sister, and the first Earl of Snowdon, Antony Armstrong-Jones.

He was born on 3rd November 1961 and he has a younger sister Lady Sarah Chatto.

He married The Honourable Serena Stanhope in 1993.

 She's the daughter of the then Viscount Petersham, now the 12th Earl of Harrington.

They have two children, The Honourable Charles Armstrong-Jones and The Honourable Margarita Armstrong-Jones.

Viscount Linley will become the second earl and Charles will presumably take the title Viscount Linley at the same time.

Margarita will change from The Honourable Margarita to Lady Margarita.

Viscount Linley is known professionally as David Linley and as a skilled craftsman he made bespoke furniture through his own company.

On 1st December 2006 he was confirmed as the chairman of Christies U.K., the auctioneers.

He has also written books and lectured around the world.

Viscount Severn is the son of H.R.H. Prince Edward, Earl of Wessex.

He was born on 17th December 2007 and he uses his father's title of Viscount as a courtesy title.

He is the youngest grandchild of Queen Elizabeth II and H.R.H. Prince Philip.

He, his parents and his sister live at Bagshot Park in Surrey, built for Charles I and once the home to Queen Victoria's son Prince Arthur of Connaught and Strathearn.

In 2008 a lake was named in his honour, Lord Severn, in Manitoba, Canada.

Lady Louise, Viscount Severn's sister also had a lake named after her in the province.

Their father was on an official tour there.

Prince Rupert of Teck, the eldest son of Prince Alexander of Teck was given the courtesy title of Viscount Trematon in 1917.

His father became the Earl of Athlone and Viscount Trematon when he renounced his German titles.

The Viscount had a short life.

He was born on 24th August 1907 at Claremont House in Esher, Surrey.

He suffered from haemophilia and he died after fracturing his skull in a car crash in France on 15th April 1928. He was twenty years old.

His father, Prince Alexander of Teck had married Princess Alice of Albany on 4th February 1904.

Princess Alice was the daughter of Prince Leopold, Duke of Albany, the youngest son of Queen Victoria.

Leopold had died in March 1884 at the age of thirty from haemophilia; Alice was a carrier of the disease which only affects males.

Rupert had an elder sister Princess Mary of Teck who became

Lady May Cambridge in 1917 and a younger brother who died in infancy named Maurice.

The Earl of Athlone, the owner of the title Viscount Trematon died in January 1957 and so too did his titles.

Non Royal Viscounts

In early 2015 there were one hundred and fifteen viscounts excluding courtesy or secondary titles and approximately two hundred and seventy including them.

English viscounts can be named after a place, use their surname or a combination of the two.
Scottish viscounts are usually designated a location.

The premier English viscount is Viscount Hereford. The title was created in 1550 for Walter Devereux, 9th Baron Ferrers of Chartley.
The second Viscount Hereford was created the Earl of Essex in 1572 but the viscountancy remained.
The third Earl of Essex, fourth Viscount Hereford, died during the English Civil War without an heir.
Whilst the title of Earl of Essex died with him the viscountcy transferred to his first cousin twice removed, Walter
and he became the fifth viscount.

The current and nineteenth Viscount Hereford is Charles Robin de Bohun Devereux.

As Robin Hereford he works for Bonhams Auctioneers.

The premier Scottish Viscount is Viscount of Falkland, usually referred to as Viscount Falkland.

Sir Henry Cary was created the first Viscount of Falkland in the Scottish Peerage in 1620.

Interestingly Cary was not Scottish nor connected to Scotland in any way.

The name comes from a royal residence, Falkland Palace in Falkland, Fife, Scotland.

The Palace is now in the care of the National Trust For Scotland.

The Falkland Islands were named after the fifth Viscount Falkland, Anthony Cary, the then Treasurer of the Navy.

The current and fifteenth Viscount Falkland is Lucius Cary, a British politician born in 1935.

His eldest son and the heir, Lucius, is known as Alexander, he is the Master of Falkland.

Alexander is a screenwriter and producer.

Viscount Gormanston is the premier viscount in Ireland, it is the oldest viscountancy in Britain and Ireland.

It was created in 1478 for Robert Preston, the son of the third Baron of Gormanston, Christopher Preston.

Since the fourteenth viscount who succeeded his father in 1876 all of the Viscount Gormanston's have been named Jenico Preston (with differing middle names.) Their heir presumptive to the title is also a Jenico.

The current and seventeenth viscount was born in 1939, he ascended to the title before he was one year old. His father, the sixteenth viscount died at Dunkirk in World War Two.

Lucy, Viscountess Gormanston, his second wife, is the daughter of the actors Edward Fox and the late Tracy Reed.

There is also a Viscount of Jersey/Vicomte de Jersey. It is a non-hereditary role that encompasses justice and entitles the holder to act as a coroner in the event of a sudden death on the island.

The Viscount of Jersey since 12th November 1981 has been Mr. Michael Wilkins M.B.E.

Many viscountcies are held by the heir to an earldom or marquessate.

An example of this is the Marquess of Salisbury, he is also the Earl of Salisbury, his heir bears the title of Viscount Cranborne rather than the Earldom.

It is dependent on family tradition and precedence.

Forms Of Address

In conversation a British viscount should be addressed as Lord and the viscountess as Lady.

Formally, a viscount is titled as The Viscount...

Their children are called The Honourable.

For example, Harold (Jonathon) Harmsworth, the fourth Viscount Rothermere has five children, all are The Honourable

–

The Honourable Vere, Eleanor, Theodora, Iris and Alfred.

Vere is the heir to the viscountcy.

Coronet

The coronet of a viscount has sixteen silver pearls around its rim, and as with other ranks of the peerage the image of the coronet may be used on a coat of arms. This image would by tradition show nine of the silver pearls.

Spotlight

Viscount Astor of Hever Castle in the County of Kent was a title created in 1917 for William Waldorf Astor, 1st Baron Astor. He had become the baron in 1916.

His eldest son, Waldorf, married Nancy Astor, she was the first woman to sit in the House of Commons. They were the second Viscount and Viscountess.

Their grandson, William Waldorf Astor III is the 4th Viscount Astor, his son, the Honourable William Waldorf Astor IV is the heir apparent to the title and his grandson, another William Waldorf (V) is next in line.

The 4th Viscount is a businessman, he holds directorships and trustee positions in companies and as an elected hereditary peer he has a seat in the House of Lords.

He married Annabel Jones in 1976.

Her stepfather was his uncle, Michael Langhorne Astor.

Annabel is the mother of Samantha Cameron, the Prime

Minister's wife.

The family seat is at Ginge Manor near to Wantage in Oxfordshire. The Astor's once lived at Cliveden in Taplow, Buckinghamshire, where three Viscounts were buried.
The Astor's gave Cliveden to the National Trust in 1942 but they continued to live there until 1968, just after the Profumo scandal had rocked politics.

It is now a five star hotel.

Viscount Churchill of Rolleston in the County of Leicester is a title held by the Spencer family. It was created in 1902 for Victor Spencer, 3rd Baron Churchill who was a Conservative politician.

In 1815 his grandfather, Lord Francis Alemeric Spencer, the younger son of the 4th Duke of Marlborough, had been created Baron Churchill of Wychwood in the County of Oxford.

He too had enjoyed a political career.

These titles are held today by the 3rd Viscount Churchill, born in 1934 but there is no heir to the viscountcy.

The title, should circumstances remain as they are, will go to the Viscount's second cousin, once removed, Richard Harry Ramsay Spencer, born in 1926.

His claim exists via the third son of the first Baron Churchill.

Notable Refusals

Arthur Henderson, a politician, was offered the title of Viscount in 1931 from Ramsay McDonald.

He declined. Ramsay MacDonald apparently wanted the competition removed to make his Labour Party leadership campaign easier. (A peer could not compete for the political position.)

Chapter 5 – Barons

Barons form the lowest rank in the hereditary peerage.

Origins and History

England

The title of baron was derived from the Latin word *baro* which translated in to old French as *baron*. This meant servant, mercenary and soldier.

The old English version was *beorn*.

Baronis was the term given to a Tenant In Chief during the early years of Norman rule.

William I (The Conqueror) was the first king to introduce barons.

In the feudal system in England it denoted loyalty to the king.

Barons took the King to be their overlord and they were barons of the king, *barones regis*.

In the feudal hierarchy beneath the barons were the knights who fought for the barons and below them, the serfs, peasants who worked the land for the knights.

The Magna Carta of 1215 was created by twenty five barons who opposed King John's blatant abuse of power. The Magna Carta was meant to ensure his compliance to the barons' rules, by force if necessary.

Luckily, the King signed the charter.

He could have declared the document illegal but he presumably realised that he would have been at the baron's mercy.

It's believed that twenty five barons were chosen because it was an odd number and therefore a deciding vote could be achieved.

Also, twenty five was a prominent number in the Bible, the link to religion would have been vital in that era.

The City of London's aldermen also numbered twenty five at

that time.

The present Court of Aldermen in the City of London has twenty five members.

During Henry II's reign the distinction was made between barons who had achieved the rank thanks to their military service and those who held land and manors.

Lords of the Manor were barons but they were deemed to be less grand than the military barons.

The most powerful barons were summoned to the King's Council which over centuries evolved into parliament and the House of Lords.

The less grand barons would receive summons to the King's Council via a sheriff and representatives of a group of barons would attend the council.

These men were elected as Knights of the Shire and they were presided over by the sheriff.

This practice developed and led to what is now the House of

Commons.

Baronies were created by a writ of summons in medieval times, this was a directive that a certain man should attend the King's Council.
Later, the creation of barons was via a letters patent of the Great Seal.

As time elapsed land would not automatically be attached to the title.

Scotland

In Scotland barons date back to the ancient nobility and the feudal system.
The Court of Lord Lyon's role was to officially recognise barons and issue them with the right to arms and a helmet that denoted their rank in the Scottish peerage.

Scottish barons are a rank below that of a Lord of Parliament. The Scottish Lord of Parliament is of an equivalent rank to an English baron.

A passport issued to a Scottish baron will be issued showing their title only if evidence from Lord Lyon's court can be sourced or the title is recognised in Burke's Peerage.

Royal Barons

Baronies are often held by members of the royal family as subsidiary titles.

Prince Charles is Baron of Renfrew, this title is closely associated with another of his Scottish titles, Duke of Rothesay.

The barony was created in 1398.

Its use as a title to the heir to the throne in Scotland was formalised in 1469 when the Baron of Renfrew was James Stewart (later King James IV,) son of King James III of Scotland.

It's believed that when the future Edward VII and Edward VIII travelled they used Lord Renfrew as a name to maintain their privacy.

Prince Philip, the Duke of Edinburgh, among his numerous honours and titles is Baron Greenwich of Greenwich in the city of London, a title which he has held since 1947.

Prince William, the Duke of Cambridge also took the titles of Baron Carrickfergus and Earl of Strathearn when he married in April 2011.

Prince Andrew became the Duke of York, Earl of Inverness and Baron Killyleagh on 23rd July 1986 when he married Sarah Ferguson.

Prince Edward, the Duke of Kent holds the title of Baron Downpatrick, this is being used by his grandson, Edward. This Edward is the son of George, the Earl of St. Andrews and heir to the dukedom.

Likewise, Xan, Baron Culloden, the eldest grandson of Prince Richard, Duke of Gloucester uses his grandfather's barony as his title.

Non Royal Barons

The premier barons in England are the Mowbray's.

Baron Mowbray was a title created in the English peerage in 1283 for Roger de Mowbray. He was summoned to parliament by King Edward I.

It was held with the title of Barony of Segrave from 1368, the fourth Baron Mowbray married Elizabeth de Segrave and their eldest son was the 5th Baron Mowbray, 1st Earl of Nottingham and 6th Baron Segrave.

He died aged seventeen and his younger brother took the titles.

The sixth Baron Mowbray, first Duke of Norfolk married Lady Elizabeth Fitzalan as his second wife.

The last Duke of Norfolk to hold the barony was the ninth Duke and twentieth Baron.

He died in 1777 without issue, his brother became the Duke of Norfolk but the line of Baron Mowbray's went in to abeyance, i.e. it was suspended.

The titles of twenty third Baron Mowbray, twenty fourth Baron Segrave were taken in 1878 by the twentieth Baron Stourton, Alfred Stourton, who was a descendant of an heiress to the baronies.

Edward Stourton is the twenty seventh Baron Mowbray, twenty eighth Baron Segrave and twenty fourth Baron Stourton.
The Honourable James Stourton, his son, is the heir to these titles.

The premier barons of Scotland were the Lord's Seton between 1371 and 1600.
In 1600 Robert Seton was created the first Earl of Winton. He was the son of the seventh Lord Seton.
Robert had supported Mary, Queen of Scots and he was a friend of the young James VI of Scotland, I of England.

He died in 1603.

His youngest daughter, Isobel, married Francis Stewart, the great nephew of the fourth Earl of Bothwell who was rumoured to have murdered Lord Darnley, James VI (I) father.

The premier baron in Ireland is Baron Kingsale.

The barony was created circa 1223 by writ although it was formalised by a letters patent in 1397.

Nevison Mark de Courcy is the thirty sixth Baron Kingsale who is a descendant of the twentieth baron.

The thirty fifth baron died in September 2005, he had not married and had no issue.

A number of baronies can be inherited by females.

For instance the Barons Whartons, at present Myles Robertson is twelfth Baron Wharton, the title will pass to the Honourable Meghan Robertson. Before Myles it was held by

Myrtle Olive Robertson, the eleventh baroness.

Forms of Address

England

Barons are The Right Honourable The Lord and their wives are The Right Honourable, The Lady.

In conversation they would be addressed as Lord and Lady. "Your Lordship" and "Your Ladyship" are acceptable as is "My Lord" but "My Lady" is not unless the Baroness is a judge by profession.

Women who hold baronies in their own right are referred to as The Right Honourable, The Baroness …or The Right Honourable, The Lady…
The title of baron does not transfer to their spouse.

A courtesy title of baron does not have the prefix of The Right Honourable. They are Lord or Lady.

Baron's children are titled The Honourable...

Scotland

Scottish barons are like clan chiefs in that they use their surnames and the territory that their barony accompanies. e.g Thomas Crawfurd of Cartsburn, 1st Baron of Cartburn.

They are formally referred to as The Much Honoured Baron. Their wives are termed Lady or The Baroness of e.g. Cartburn. It should be noted that calling a Baroness Lady would be incorrect unless they hold the barony in their own right.

In speech you can call barons Baron or use their territory name.

Coronet

A baron or baroness is entitled to a coronet with six silver pearls around the ring.

Unlike the higher ranks in the peerage the rim of the coronet is not adorned with jewels.

The coronet may be shown on a coat of arms above the shield with four of the silver pearls visible.

Scottish feudal barons coats of arms depict the baron's helmet. The steel helmet has three gold grilles.

They may also have a chapeau or a red cap which holds no silver balls or gilt decoration. This was a recent invention used for coats of arms from the 1930's in to this century.

Spotlight

The first Baron Tweedsmuir of Elsfield in the county of Oxford was the author and politician John Buchan.

The title was created in 1935 and he was the Governor-General of Canada from 1935 until his death five years later.

Tweedsmuir was a village in the Scottish Borders close to where he had grown up.

The title passed to his eldest son and it is currently held by John William de l'Aigle Buchan, the 4th Baron, the second Baron's nephew.

He acquired the title in 2008.

The Honourable James Buchan, the younger son of the third Baron Tweesmuir is an author.

The title of Baron Montagu of Beaulieu in the County of Hampshire was created in 1885 for Lord Henry Montagu Douglas Scott, the second son of the 5th Duke of Buccleuch.

The Baron was a Conservative politician.

When Henry Montagu Douglas Scott was created Baron Montagu he changed his and his descendant's surnames to Douglas Scott Montagu.

Edward Douglas Scott Montagu is the third Baron and he has held the title since 1929, when he was two years old.
He founded the National Motor Museum on his Beaulieu estate.
He resides at the Palace House at Beaulieu, the house was built around the gatehouse of the ruined monastery of Beaulieu Abbey.
He is one of the elected hereditary peers in the House of Lords.

The heir is his son the Honourable Ralph Douglas Scott Montagu.

Her Royal Highness Princess Alice, Duchess of Gloucester

1901-2004, was born Alice Montagu Douglas Scott, the sister to the 8th Duke of Buccleuch.

Her first cousin was Sarah, Duchess of York's grandmother, Marion Montagu Douglas Scott.

The Barons of Beaulieu are in the line of succession for the Dukedoms of Queensbury and Buccleuch, held by Richard Scott, the current Duke and head of Clan Scott.

Baron Kensington is a title that has been created three times in different peerages.

Its first incarnation was in 1623 in the peerage of England for Henry Rich, a younger son of the Earl of Warwick.

The fifth Baron Kensington died in 1759 and this and the other titles the family had achieved became extinct.

The title was recreated in 1776 in the peerage of Scotland for Lady Elizabeth Rich and Francis Edwardes' son William.

William Edwardes, the fourth Baron Kensington was made Baron Kensington of Kensington in the County of Middlesex in the peerage of the United Kingdom in 1886.

Today the title is held by Hugh Edwardes, the eighth Baron Kensington, born in 1933.
He has held the title since 1981. His uncle William Edwardes was his predecessor.

The Duke of Brandon and Hamilton holds the title of Baron Dutton in the County of Chester.
This title was created in September 1711 with the dukedom of Brandon, both were titles in the peerage of Great Britain for the fourth Duke of Hamilton in the Scottish peerage after his influential work on the Act of Union 1707.

Sir James Abercrombie was an illegitimate son of the fourth Duke, he was known as Sir James Abercrombie, 1st Baronet of Edinburgh.

He died in 1724 without issue.

Notable Refusals

George Macaulay Booth, the son of the Right Honourable Charles Booth was Director of the Bank of England, High Sheriff of London (1936) and Lieutenant of the City of London. He refused the title of baron from David Lloyd George.

Sir Alan Lascelles, known as Tommy Lascelles, was the Private Secretary to George VI and Elizabeth II.

He declined a barony in 1953. He felt that titles displayed a person's feeling of self importance.

He did accept Knight Grand Cross of the Order of the Bath, Knight Grand Cross of the Royal Victorian Order and Companion of the Order of St. Michael and St. George.

He also held several military medals and honours.

Chapter 6- More Extinct Titles

Extinct Royal Dukedoms

Duke of Albany

Duke of Albemarle

Duke of Bedford

Duke of Windsor

Duke of Hereford

Duke of Kendal

Duke of Sussex

There was a tradition with the Hanoverian monarchs to add two dukedoms together for a title, one English and the other Scottish, it helped to reinforce the notion of a United Kingdom.

Duke of Gloucester and Edinburgh

Duke of Cumberland and Strathearn

Duke of York and Albany

Duke of Kent and Strathearn

Duke of Cumberland and Teviotdale

Duke of Clarence and Avondale

Duke of Clarence and St. Andrews

Duke of Connaught and Strathearn

The dukedoms of Albany and Cumberland and Teviotdale
were suspended in 1919 as a result of the Great War.
The Dukes had fought with Germany and they held German
titles, respectively the Duke of Saxe Coburg-Gotha and the
Elector of Hanover.
Heirs to these titles are alive and they can apply for the titles
to be restored.
Hanover has allegedly made unsuccessful attempts at this.

The Scottish Duke of Kintyre and Lorne, Marquess of Wigton,
Earl of Carrick and Lord Annandale was the fifth son of James
VI of Scotland (James I of England) and Anne of Denmark.
Robert Bruce Stuart was born on the 18th January 1602. He

was given his titles on 2nd May 1602 and he died on 27th May 1602.

The titles, only in use for twenty five days, died with him.

The title of Duke of Windsor was bestowed on King Edward VIII after his abdication in 1936. It was a bitter fact to him that while he possessed the prefix of His Royal Highness, Wallis, Duchess of Windsor was never given the H.R.H.

Non Royal Titles

The title of Duke of Portland is the most recent dukedom to become extinct. It ceased in 1990 but the Earldom of Portland still exists and is currently held by the actor Timothy Bentinck.

The title of Duke of Buckingham has been created seven times. The Villiers family as Dukes of Buckingham played a large part in history particularly in Stuart times.

Richard Plantagenet Campbell Temple-Nugent-Brydges-Chandos-Grenville, the 3rd Duke of Buckingham and Chandos, 7th Viscount Cobham died in 1889. He had no male issue and the title transferred as a subsidiary title to a distant relation, the Baron Lyttleton, who became the 8th Viscount Cobham.

The prominent politician and Viceroy of India George Nathaniel Curzon (1859-1925) was known by several titles, this is a selection of them.

1859 The Hon. George Nathaniel Curzon

1886 The Hon. George Nathaniel Curzon M.P.

1898 The Right Honourable The Lord Curzon of Kedleston (Baron Curzon of Kedleston.)

He was given the titles Knight Grand Commander (GCSI) and Knight Commander (GCIE) of the Order of the Star of India in 1899. He sat on the Privy Council (PC) from 1901 and was awarded the Order of the Garter in 1916 (KG)

1911 The Rt Hon. The Earl Curzon of Kedleston GCSI, GCIE, PC

1916 The Rt Hon. The Earl Curzon of Kedleston KG, GCSI, GCIE, PC

1921–1925 death: The Most Hon. The Marquess Curzon of Kedleston KG, GCSI, GCIE, PC

The Marquessate of Ormonde ceased in 1997.

James Hubert Theobald Charles Butler, 7th Marquess of Ormonde was the last holder of the title.

He had daughters but no sons and the title of Earl of Ormonde is currently dormant. The earldom could be claimed by the 18th Viscount Mountgarret. So far it has not been claimed successfully.

Today, we have the Marquessate of Bath, the 7th marquess is Alexander George Thynn, born in 1932. The 1st Marquess of Bath was Thomas Thynne, 3rd Viscount Weymouth. The marquess also holds Baron Thynne as a title.

The marquessate is completely unrelated to an earldom that became extinct during its fifth creation.

The earldom of Bath was created three times in the English peerage, once in the Peerage of Great Britain and once in the Peerage of the United Kingdom.

The first creation was in 1486 for Philibert de Chandee, the second in 1536 for the Bourchier's, the third in 1661 for the Granville's, the fourth in 1742 for William Pulteney and the last creation was in 1803 when Henrietta Laura Pulteney held the title of Countess of Bath until her death in 1808.

It was surprising that the marquessate and the earldom were in existence at the same time, a duplication of places in the peerage is rare.

Interestingly, it has been suggested that the Dukes of Devonshire who reside at Chatsworth House in Derbyshire, were meant to be titled the Dukes of Derbyshire because the Earls of Devon already existed at the time of the dukedoms creation.

The earldom of Kent has been created nine times in its history. Firstly, in 1020 it was created for Godwin of Wessex, he was the father of Harold Godwinson or King Harold II who was killed at the Battle of Hastings in 1066.
The earldom was not Harold's it belonged to his brother Leofwine who also died at this battle.

In 1067 William I - the Conqueror – gave the title to his half brother Odo.

Odo was killed on his way to the First Crusade in 1097 although he had forfeited the title in 1088.

The third incarnation was for William of Ypres in 1141, however, he lost the title in 1155.

Fourthly was Hubert de Burgh in 1227. He died in 1243.

Next, the earldom was recreated in 1321 for Edmund of Woodstock, the title passed to his son Edmund and then through John and on to his sister Joan, 4th Countess of Kent in 1352.

The sixth version of 1360 was created for the husband of the Joan above, Thomas Holland. He died the same year.

The second and third earls in this creation were also Thomas Holland's.

The last earl was Edmund Holland who died in battle 15th September 1408.

The seventh creation was in 1461 for William Neville. His mother Joan of Beaufort was a legitimised daughter of John of Gaunt, the first Duke of Lancaster and Katherine Swynford. He died in 1463.

The eighth creation was for the Grey family.

Edmund Grey was made the first Earl of Kent in 1465.

The line changed with Henry Grey, the twelfth earl. In 1706 he became Marquess of Kent and in 1710 this became a dukedom. His children predeceased him and the title became extinct when he died in 1740.

Lastly, the ninth incarnation was for Prince Alfred, Duke of Edinburgh and Saxe Coburg Gotha.

He was the second son of Queen Victoria and Prince Albert.

Alfred died in 1900, his only son, also Alfred had died in 1899. The earldom became extinct.

His nephew Prince Charles of Albany took the Saxe Coburg Gotha title only.

Kent was revived, but as a dukedom in 1934 for Prince George, the fourth son of King George V.

The Viscounts of Dundee were short lived in the Scottish peerage.

John Graham, the 7th Laird of Claverhouse was made Lord Graham of Claverhouse and 1st Viscount Dundee on 12th November 1688.

He remained loyal to James VII of Scotland (II of England) in 1688 after the Glorious Revolution.

He lost his life in the battle at Killiecrankie but his army was victorious.

He became a Jacobite hero and was given the name "Bonnie Dundee" as a tribute.

The 2nd Viscount Dundee was James Graham, he died in 1689 and the 3rd Viscount of Dundee, David Graham, died in 1700.

The third viscount had lost the titles in 1699.

The title became extinct and it has not been recreated.

Chapter 7 - Life Peers

Origins and History

Between 1603, the start of James I's reign and 1760, the end of George II's reign, eighteen life peerages were created for women.

Women were not permitted to sit in the House of Lords and it was not evident whether a man who was given a life peerage was eligible to sit there either.

In 1856 a legal expert was installed in the House of Lords, it was also the final court of appeal.

It transpired that the judge in question was not permitted to sit in the House of Lords so he was given a hereditary peerage so that he could.

Baron Wensleydale, as he became, had no heir to pass his hereditary title to.

In 1869 Earl Russell proposed a bill that decreed that there could only be twenty eight life peers at any time

Moreover, no more than four life peers could be created in a year and these life peers would be chosen by senior judges, officials and peers from Ireland and Scotland.

Earl Russell's bill was rejected by the House of Lords.

The Appellate Jurisdiction Act of 1876 permitted senior judges to attend the House of Lords as life peers or "Lords of Appeal In Ordinary."

However, the Supreme Court of the United Kingdom was created by the Constitutional Reform Act of 2005 and this tradition ended.

Non hereditary life peers are created in accordance with the Life Peerages Act 1958.

The act removed the limit to the number of peers that a monarch could create and it gave life peers the right, once they were aged twenty one, resident in the U.K. for tax purposes and if they'd not committed a crime, to sit in the House of Lords.

This was the first time that women had the right to sit in the House.

Hereditary peeresses did not enjoy this privilege until 1963.

The House of Lords Act 1999 meant that the number of hereditary peers who had a seat in the House of Lords was dramatically reduced.

Ninety two hereditary peers including the Earl Marshal and the Lord Great Chamberlain were permitted and ten hereditary peers received life peerages so that they were not excluded from the House of Lords.

For example, George Jellicoe, 2nd Earl Jellicoe was created Baron Jellicoe of Southampton and David Hennessy, 3rd Baron Windlesham was created Baron Hennessy of Windlesham.

In late 1999 there had been one thousand three hundred and thirty members of the House of Lords but by spring 2000 it was six hundred and sixty nine and life peers far outnumbered the hereditary peers.

Prior to the 2010 General Election the Labour Party had proposed that the ninety two hereditary heirs should be phased out gradually.

Labour did not return to power after the election and the Conservative/Liberal Democrat coalition government have not pursued their opponent's idea.

A life peer may take their surname e.g. Baroness Warnock and Baron Bell.

They can add a location e.g. Baroness Masham of Ilton and Baron Harris of Haringey.

Some choose not to use their surname; John Selwyn Gummer took the title of Baron Deben.

The Present Day

The Prime Minister proposes who should be considered for a life peerage and the Queen gives her assent or veto as appropriate.

Life peerages are announced on the following occasions:

The New Year's Honours.

The Queen's Birthday Honours.

The Resignation Honours - when a Prime Minister reaches the end of their time in office.

The Dissolution Honours which marks the dissolution of parliament.

The recipients are often leading figures in their field.

The House of Lords has approximately seven hundred and sixty peers at the moment and the majority of them are life peers.

To date all of the life peers have been created barons.

Prime Ministers David Cameron and Tony Blair have created the most life peers while in office. Cameron's total is forty one, Blair's was thirty six life peers per year.

Life peers do not receive a salary unless they hold a ministerial role.
There is a travel and accommodation allowance of £300 per day should a life peer wish to attend the House of Lords but there is no legal requirement for them to do so.

Working Peers represent the various political parties.
The Prime Minister and the leaders of the opposition parties are allowed a certain number of these life peers at any one time.

Since 2000 The House of Lords Appointments Commission has created what have become known as *The People's Peers*. People contact the commission with their nominations.

Prior to 2000 it was the Prime Minister who nominated the candidates.

Since the Peerage Act 1963 hereditary peers could disclaim their title for their lifetime.

It was 2014 before life peers were accorded the right to resign.

Forms of Address

Life peers can be referred to as The Noble Lord as they would be if they were a hereditary peer.

More commonly they are formally addressed as The Right Honourable the Lord or Baroness...

Informally they are called Lord/Baroness/Lady.

The children of life peers are titled The Honourable, as if they were the issue of a hereditary peer but they don't inherit their parent's title.

Spotlight

Sebastian Coe, the former Conservative politician and athlete who headed the successful bid and committee for London's 2012 Summer Olympics, was made a life peer on 16th May 2000 with the title of Baron Coe of Ranmore in the County of Surrey.

He has several honours. He was given an M.B.E. in 1982 and an O.B.E. in 1990, he was appointed Knight Commander of the Order of the British Empire (K.B.E.) in 2006 and in 2013 he was appointed to the Order of the Companions of Honour (C.H.)

Julian Fellowes is a screenwriter, director and possibly best known as the creator of Downton Abbey. He was created a life peer on 12th January 2011 as Baron Fellowes of West Stafford in the County of Dorset.
He sits on the Conservative benches in the House of Lords.

He married Emma Kitchener.

In 1998 they changed their name from Fellowes to Kitchener-Fellowes.

Their son is The Honourable Peregrine Kitchener-Fellowes.

Emma was a lady in waiting to H.R.H. Princess Michael of Kent and she holds the Royal Victorian Order.

She is the great grand-niece of Field Marshal Kitchener, 1st Earl Kitchener, the Secretary of State for War in the First World War, until his death in 1916.

The earldom became extinct with no males to inherit it.

In May 2012 the Queen issued a warrant to allow Emma Kitchener-Fellowes the same privileges as the daughter of an earl.

Had the hereditary rules been different she would have been the fourth Countess Kitchener.

Sir Alec Douglas-Home, the former Prime Minister was given a life peerage.

He had renounced his hereditary title of the Earl of Home to pursue politics.

He was the first former Prime Minister to accept a life peerage.

Prime Ministers Wilson, Callaghan and Thatcher accepted life peerages. Former Chancellors of the Exchequer, and high ranking ministers and officials have also taken them.

Retired Archbishops of Canterbury and York may also be made life peers.

Every Archbishop of Canterbury since 1958 has become a life peer.

Notable Refusals

John Cleese, the actor and comedian was offered a life peerage in 1999 but he apparently called this "silly." He had refused a C.B.E. in 1996.

Sir Edward Heath, another former Prime Minister declined a life peerage for two known reasons.
He disapproved of political honours whilst being aware that they were a good way to garner support for your party and he preferred to be a Member of Parliament.

J.B. Priestley the author and playwright refused a life peerage in 1965.
He accepted the Order of Merit on 24th October 1977.

George Woodcock, General Secretary of the Trade Union Congress (T.U.C.) did not take a life peerage in 1970 because the honour went against his socialist principles.

Prince Philip, Prince Charles, Prince Andrew, Prince Edward, Prince Richard (Gloucester) and Prince Edward (Kent) could have taken life peerages after the House of Lords reforms in 1999.

They all declined.

Part Two - Chivalric Orders

The Order Of The Garter

The Most Ancient and Most Noble Order of the Thistle

The Most Honourable Order of the Bath

The Most Distinguished Order of St. Michael and St. George

Royal Victorian Order

The Order of Merit

Imperial Service Order

The Most Excellent Order of the British Empire: G.B.E, K.B.E. and D.B.E.

The Most Excellent Order of the British Empire: C.B.E., M.B.E. and O.B.E.

The Order of Companions of Honour

Chapter 8 - The Order Of The Garter

About The Order

This is the oldest and most senior Order of Chivalry in the nation; the Order of the Garter was founded by King Edward III in 1348.

Historians have surmised that Edward III wished to install a group reminiscent of King Arthur's Knights of the Round Table around him.

Another theory of how the order started is that Edward was dancing when his partner's blue garter fell to the floor, he picked it up and placed it around his own leg using the phrase "Honi soit qui mal y pense."

In English this means "shame on him who thinks this evil."

The lady has never been identified but Edward III's cousin, Joan, known as the Fair Maid of Kent, Queen Philippa of

Hainault or Katherine, Countess of Salisbury are considered to be the most probable dance partners.

There was a lavish feast and jousting to celebrate the creation of the Order of the Garter.
"Honi soit qui mal y pense" became the order's motto.

The use of the phrase in French could also have referred to Edward III's claim to the French throne and the order as a way to win support.

Charles I wore his Order of the Garter to his execution in 1649. It was decorated with over four hundred diamonds.

Disregarding the reigning queen's, until Queen Alexandra, Edward VII's wife received the Order of the Garter in 1901 the last female to hold the honour was Henry VII's mother, Margaret Beaufort.
She died in 1509.

Women, other than wives of King's, were not given the honour until 1987.

From the eighteenth century until 1946 parliament was consulted about appointments to the order.
Since that time the order has been solely a Royal honour.

The patron saint of the Order is St. George and St. George's Chapel at Windsor is its spiritual home.
Each knight has an enamelled stall-plate and their banner of arms on display in St. George's Chapel. This is in addition to a helmet, their crest and sword.

On the death of one of the knight's these items and the insignia are returned to the monarch.
The stall plate remains in St. George's Chapel, the oldest plates date back to circa 1390.
There is no other collection of stall plates like this in the world.

The Order has the monarch at its head and twenty four knights, termed as Companions. Originally, the monarch had twelve companions and the Prince of Wales had another twelve as if they were in teams.

The Companion Knights are selected on merit.

They are people who have served the monarch personally, held public office or enhanced the lives of others.

The monarch holds the right to appoint additional members of royalty, British and foreign. These are known as Supernumerary Knights and Ladies.

Currently, the Queen and Prince Charles hold the Order of the Garter as the monarch and the Prince of Wales.

The other British royal holders of the honour are H.R.H. The Duke of Edinburgh, H.R.H. The Duke of Kent, H.R.H. The Duke of Gloucester, H.R.H. Princess Alexandra, The Hon. Lady Ogilvy, H.R.H. The Duke of York, H.R.H. Anne, The Princess Royal, H.R.H. The Earl of Wessex and H.R.H. The Duke of Cambridge.

Extra Knights can be monarchs from other countries; the Kings of Spain and Norway are currently Extra Knights.

Each June on the Monday of Royal Ascot week the Knights of the Garter visit Windsor Castle where the new Knights participate in a ceremony in which they take the oath and accept the insignia of the order.
Luncheon is then served in the magnificent Waterloo Chamber at Windsor.

In the afternoon there is a procession from the castle to St. George's Chapel.
The Knights and Ladies are accompanied by the monarch and other royal holders of the order.

Males are Knights Companion and females are Ladies Companion.
They use either the letters K.G. or L.G. after their names.

Current Knights and Ladies Companion's include The Duke of Abercorn, who also holds the office of the Chancellor of the Order, The Admiral of the Fleet, The Lord Boyce and Field Marshals, The Lord Inge and The Lord Bramall.

At the time of writing there are three positions vacant. New appointments are announced on St. George's Day, the 23rd April.

Robes And Insignia

The original manner of displaying the order's insignia was a garter and a badge which showed St. George and the Dragon. In the sixteenth century a collar was added and in the seventeenth, a ribbon and star were created.

The dark blue mantle was once made from wool but has been velvet since the 1500's.
The lining is taffeta. The right shoulder bears a red hood which is seldom (possibly never) worn in contemporary times.
The black hat is Tudor by design and is velvet with white ostrich and black heron feathers.

The collar is solid gold. It is formed by gold knots and enamelled roses surrounded by the garter in an alternating pattern.
A "George" the representation of St. George is worn from the collar.

The dark blue buckled garter may be worn on the left leg by men and on the left arm by the ladies.

Interestingly, until the latter half of the twentieth century the undergarments worn on ceremonial occasions were in the Tudor style.
That apparently does not happen now except at Coronations by canopy holders.

The star was introduced by King Charles I and it is worn on the left side of the chest.
It shows an enamelled shield of St. George's Cross encircled by the garter.
The garter is surrounded by an eight pointed silver badge.
Four of the points are longer than the other four.
Each point is shown as a number of rays.

As the premier honour in Great Britain this star would be worn above any others that the wearer might possess.

Notable Refusal

Sir Winston Churchill was offered the Order of the Garter in 1945.

With the Second World War won the electorate voted him out of office.

It's been reported that he declined commenting that "I can hardly accept the Order of the Garter from the King after the people have given me the Order of the Boot."

He did accept the honour in 1953, the middle year of his second term as Prime Minister and the year that he won the Nobel Prize for Literature.

Chapter 9 – The Most Ancient and Most Noble Order of the Thistle

About The Order

It is Scotland's highest honour and only the Order of the Garter - United Kingdom outranks it.

The order is given to Scots who have held public office or contributed greatly to the national way of life.

Its exact date of creation is unknown although there is a legend that King Achaius of the Scots made an alliance with the Emperor Charlemagne in 809 A.D. and that it was at this point in time that the order was invented.

Another legend, that King Achaius created it in 786 A.D. after seeing the cross of St. Andrew in the sky when he was fighting a battle against the Saxon king Aethelstan of East Anglia has been discredited; Aethelstan was not born until either 893 or 895 A.D.

It's also been suggested that Robert the Bruce created the honour at the Battle of Bannockburn in June 1314. The battle was a huge success for the Scots.

James III of Scotland reigned 1460-1488. He was responsible for changes in the royal symbolism and that included the adoption of a thistle on coins and the royal badge.
The thistle became the national flower of Scotland.

James V is believed to have honoured King Francis I of France with the "Order of the Burr or Thissil" in 1535 but frustratingly there isn't any proof of this.

There is no record in Scottish history to confirm that the order was used until James VII of Scotland (II of England) established - or re-established - the order on 29th May 1687. The honour allowed him to reward the Scottish peers who supported his political and religious efforts.
The number of members was limited to twelve Knights

Brethren plus the monarch. This was to symbolise Jesus and the twelve apostles.

The order appears to have remained unused after James' abdication in 1688 until Queen Anne reintroduced it in 1703.

The Hanoverian kings used the order as a reward to Scottish peers who had proven that they were sympathetic to the Protestant cause and to their monarch.

George IV wore his Order of the Thistle on a visit to Scotland in 1822.

The number of members was increased to sixteen in 1827.

Extra members may be British royalty or a foreign monarch.

The monarch is the sovereign of the order.

St. Andrew is the patron saint of Scotland and of the order.

The order's motto is "Nemo me impune lacessit" which in English means "No one harms (provokes) me with impunity."

The order did not have an official spiritual home until 1911 when Thistle Chapel, St Giles' Cathedral in Edinburgh was selected.

James VII (II) had wished to use Abbey Church at the Palace of Holyroodhouse but he was deposed before this occurred.

Each of the members has an allotted stall in the Thistle Chapel and their stall plate is not removed when they die.

Since 1987 Scottish women have been eligible for the honour although George VI bestowed the order on his wife, Queen Elizabeth, the mother of the present queen, in 1937.

Princess Anne, The Princess Royal was given the order in 2001.

Current members include The Earl of Airlie, Lady Marion Frazer and The Lord Hope of Craighead.

The Lord Smith of Kelvin and The Earl of Home joined the order in 2014.

It is the monarch's choice who should receive the order and

since George VI's reign consultation with the government is not required.

If there are vacancies the new appointments are announced on St. Andrew's Day, the 30th November.

Each June or July the new members are installed by the Queen at the Palace of Holyroodhouse.

Knights use K.T. after their name, Ladies use L.T.

They are called Sir or Lady followed by their forename.

Holders of the Order of the Thistle are not excluded from the Order of the Garter but the choice to relinquish the Thistle for the Garter was made several times between 1710, Queen Anne's time, and the end of Queen Victoria's reign.

Robes And Insignia

For ceremonial occasions a green mantle is worn over a uniform or civilian clothing.

The mantle is lined with white taffeta and it is tied with gold and green tassels.

To accompany this there is a black velvet hat with white feathers and a black egret or heron's feather at the top.

The gold collar is worn over the mantle and it bears an image of thistles and sprigs of rue, also known as herb of grace.

The "St. Andrew" or badge appendant is suspended from the collar. St. Andrew is depicted in gold enamel with rays coming from his head, holding a white saltire (cross) and wearing a green gown and a purple coat.

The star of the Order of the Thistle is a silver St. Andrew's saltire.

A pointed ray of light lies between each of the arms of the cross and at the centre a gold medallion shows an enamelled thistle, the green border carries the orders motto.

The star is worn on the left shoulder of the mantle.

On more informal occasions the star may be worn with a sash of dark green placed across the body from the left shoulder to the right hip. The badge is attached at the right hip.

Members are permitted to encircle their arms with the green circlet bearing the order's motto and the collar. The badge may be shown hanging from the collar.

When a member of the Order of the Thistle dies the insignia must be returned to the Central Chancery of the Orders of Knighthood.

The badge and the star are personally presented to the monarch by the closest relative to the deceased.

Notable Refusals

I could not find any record of a person declining the honour.

Chapter 10 - The Most Honourable Order of the Bath

The Order of the Bath was the fourth most senior order in Britain.

However, the order above it The Most Illustrious Order of St. Patrick has been dormant for almost a century so it is now considered to be the third highest honour.

From its creation by George III in 1783 to 1922 The Order of St. Patrick was an honour which served Ireland in the same way that the Order of the Thistle did Scotland.

The order went in to abeyance when the Irish Free State began in 1922.

H.R.H. Prince Henry, the Duke of Gloucester had been the last person alive to hold the order, he died in 1974.

The post nominal letters had been K.P.

About the Order

The Order of the Bath was formerly known as the Most Honourable Military Order of the Bath.

It was created by George I on 18th May 1725 by a letters patent under the Great Seal.

The name was derived from the medieval ceremony for creating a knight in which the recipient would have bathed as a demonstration of their purification. These knights were known as "Knights of the Bath."

George I's Order of the Bath was not a revival of the unofficial medieval title.

The 1725 Order was official and maintained by statutes.

Robert Walpole, the nation's first Prime Minister was in power between 1721 and 1742, he used the Order of the Bath to enhance his political position by offering the order as a favour.

Until the end of the Napoleonic War there was only one rank, that of Knight Companion.

The Prince Regent, later George IV, expanded the order to honour those who had proved themselves to be exceptional in the war.

Three classes of the order were created:

Knights Grand Cross

Military members had to hold the rank of Major General, Rear Admiral or higher to be eligible for the honour.

Sixty military and twelve diplomatic or civil members were permitted.

Knights Commanders

The recipient had to be the rank of Lieutenant Colonel or Post Captain.

These were limited to one hundred and eighty.

Companions

The holder had to have been mentioned in despatches since 1803, the start of the war, or already have been awarded a medal.

There was no official limit but the first list of recipients numbered approximately five hundred.

Queen Victoria split the order in to two divisions in 1847, one military and the other civil and she introduced a formal investiture.

The Grand Master was a role that Queen Victoria merged with the position of Principal Knight Companion.

The Grand Master traditionally holds the seal of the order and he enforces the rules, he is Principal Knight Grand Cross.

Women were admitted to the order in 1971.

A member of the order and their children may marry at Westminster Abbey.

The motto of the Order of the Bath is "Tria juncta in uno" which means "three joined in one."
Its spiritual home is at Henry VII Lady Chapel in Westminster Abbey.

Here, every four years there is an installation ceremony which the Grand Master, since 1974 H.R.H. Prince Charles, presides over.
The monarch attends alternate ceremonies and Queen Elizabeth II attended the last ceremony in May 2014.
At Westminster Abbey the member's heraldic devices, banner and stall plate are displayed.

Today, the Queen, the sovereign of the order and the Prince of Wales, the Grand Master, are members.
Recipients are normally senior military officials and senior civil servants.

Honorary members may be appointed; these are Commonwealth citizens and foreigners who are not subjects of the monarch.

The monarch takes advice from the government about who should be awarded the honour.

Current Knights Grand Cross include General. The Lord Dannatt, who is the Constable of the Tower of London and General Sir Michael Jackson, a former Chief of General Staff, he had a military career that lasted for over forty five years.

Honorary Knights Grand Cross are the Presidents of France, Jacques Chirac, Nicolas Sarkozy and Francois Hollande, President of South Africa, Jacob Zuma and King Abdullah II of Jordan.

The current limits to the number of recipients are as follows:

One hundred and twenty Knights or Dames Grand Cross

Three hundred and fifty five Knights or Dames Commanders

One thousand nine hundred and twenty five Companions.

The monarch may only exceed the numerical limits in exceptional situations or in wartime.

The minimum military ranks for Knights and Dames Grand Cross are Rear Admiral, Major General or Air Vice Marshall.

Knight or Dames Commanders must have achieved the rank of Naval Captain, an Army or Royal Marine Colonel or a Group Captain in the Royal Air Force.

Companions must be Lieutenant Commander, Major, Squadron Leader or higher.
They must have been mentioned in despatches for distinguished conduct in a command position in combat and engineers and medics may be appointed for service in wartime.

Robes And Insignia

On ceremonial occasions Knights and Dames Grand Cross wear a crimson satin mantle lined with taffeta. It is held together by two large tassels.

On the left side is an image of the star of the order.

The hat worn by Knights and Dames Grand Cross and Commanders is made of black velvet and an upright plume of feathers is attached.

The collar is gold and it weighs 933 grams. The images of nine imperial crowns and eight sets of flowers are connected by seventeen silver knots.

The flowers change dependent on which country the recipient comes from, roses for England, thistles for Scotland and shamrocks for Ireland.

On "collar days" designated by the monarch the collar may be worn over a military uniform or evening wear. Whenever the collar is worn the badge is suspended from it.

On less formal occasions the star is worn by the Knights and Dames Grand Cross. It is pinned to the left breast.

Military Knights and Dames Grand Cross wear a star which consists of a Maltese cross on top of an eight pointed silver star.

There are three crowns surrounded by a red ring showing the motto of the order in gold lettering. The ring has two laurel branches and Ich dien (I serve) inscribed in gold on a scroll below.

Civil Knights and Dames Grand Cross have an eight pointed silver star with no Maltese Cross, laurel leaves or Ich dien.

Military Knights and Dames Commanders have an eight pointed silver cross pattee.

Cross pattee means that it is narrow in the centre and its arms broaden towards the edges.

The three crowns, the red ring, motto, laurel leaves and Ich dien appear.

Civil Knights and Dames Commanders have an eight pointed silver cross pattee without the laurel leaves and Ich dien.

The badges vary in size and design dependent on the holders rank and the division.
The lower the rank, the smaller the badge but they are all suspended on a crimson ribbon.

The military badge is a white enamelled eight pointed gold Maltese Cross.
Each point of the cross has a small gold ball and each angle bears the image of a lion.
The centre of the cross has three crowns on the obverse side, the reverse shows either a rose, thistle or shamrock coming from a sceptre.
Both of the emblems are surrounded by a red ring showing the motto of the order, laurel leaves and a scroll with Ich dien on it.

The civil badge is a plain gold oval with three crowns on its obverse side and either a rose, thistle or shamrock coming from a sceptre on the reverse.

Again red rings and the motto of the order are displayed.

Knights and Dames Grand Cross wear their badges on ribands or sashes from the right shoulder to the left hip.

Knights Commanders and male Companions wear the badge around the neck and their female counterparts wear the badge on a bow on the left.

Knights and Dames Grand Cross may surround their arms with a circlet bearing the order's motto, the badge pendant and the collar.

Knights and Dames Commanders and Companions may show the circlet but not the collar around their arms.

The badge of the order should be shown hanging from the collar or the circlet, as appropriate.

Military division holders may add two laurel leaves and the scroll with Ich Dien showing as it does on the badge.

Upon the death of a Knight or Dame Cross the collars and badges must be returned to the Central Chancery of the Orders of Knighthood and only the stall plate remains at the Abbey.

In 1815 it was suggested that the banner and stall plates of the Knights Commanders should be installed in the chapel too but due to a lack of space this did not happen.

Queen Victoria's amendments to the order in 1847 gave all three classes the right to request that a stall-plate be created for them.

Notable Refusal

Admiral George Cranfield Berkeley was a politician and naval officer. He lived between 1753 and 1818. He was the third son of the fourth Earl Berkeley.

He declined the Order of the Bath in 1812 allegedly because he expected a position in the peerage.

In 1813 he relented and accepted Knight Companion of the Order of the Bath.

This was upgraded to Knight Grand Cross in 1815.

He never received a peerage, much to his regret.

Chapter 11 - The Most Distinguished Order of St. Michael and St. George

The order is the fourth most senior one.

In the past the third, The Most Illustrious Order of St. Patrick 1783-1922 and the fifth highest The Most Exalted Star of India 1861 – 1947 were not dormant and this was the sixth highest honour.

The Partition of India took place in 1947 and the last awards of the Star of India were made in the New Year's Honours 1948. The last holder died in 2009.

About The Order

This order was founded on 28th April 1818 by The Prince Regent, later King George IV to celebrate the Ionian Islands including Corfu, Zakynthos and Kefalonia being placed under British protection.

It was originally intended for inhabitants of these and the Maltese islands but since 1879 people in the United Kingdom have been eligible for the order.

St. Michael and St. George are two military saints.

The order was limited to the following levels on its creation:

Fifteen Knights Grand Cross

Twenty Knights Commanders

Twenty five Companions.

Its motto is "Auspicium melioris aevi" which means "Token of a better age."

Its original spiritual home was the Palace of St. Michael and St. George in Corfu, Greece.

Since 1906 St. Paul's Cathedral in London has been its home.

Today, the order is given to diplomats and officials who serve the United Kingdom from overseas, for example, employees of the Foreign and Commonwealth Office.

There are still three classes which you may be appointed to:

Knight Grand Cross or Dame Grand Cross (G.C.M.G.)

Knight Commander (K.C.M.G.) or Dame Commander

(D.C.M.G.)

Companion (C.M.G.)

The monarch is the Sovereign of the Order and the Grand

Master since 1967 has been H.R.H Prince Edward, the Duke of

Kent.

New knights are installed in a religious ceremony held once

every four years.

The monarch and the Knights and Dames Grand Cross are

given stalls in the choir of St. Paul's Cathedral's chapel. Their

heraldic devices and stall-plates are displayed. The helms and

coronets are removed after the death of the holder but the stall

plate remains attached to the stall.

The original numerical limits have been broadened considerably to:

One hundred and twenty five Knights Grand Cross.

Three hundred and seventy five Knights Commanders.

One thousand seven hundred and fifty Companions.

Royal holders of the order, British or foreign, are not included in these numbers.

Current holders of the Order of St. Michael and St. George include:

As Knights Grand Cross

Peter Carrington, 6th Baron Carrington, a retired Conservative politician who served as Defence Secretary and Foreign Secretary during his career.

Catherine Ashton, The Baroness Ashton of Upholland is a

Labour politician who during her career has been the High Representative of the Union for Foreign Affairs and Security Policy and First Vice President of the European Commission. She was given the order in the 2015.New Years Honours.

Honorary Knights or Dames Grand Cross include:

Simon Peres, the former Israeli Prime Minister.

Henrik, the Prince Consort of Denmark, married to Queen Margarethe II.

Kofi Annan, the former Secretary General of the United Nations.

Angelina Jolie is an Honorary Dame Commander of the Order of St. Michael and St. George.

She may use the post nominals D.C.M.G.

She received the honour in 2014.

Robes And Insignia

On ceremonial occasions the Knights and Dames Grand Cross have a Saxon blue satin mantle lined with crimson silk.

It has two large tassels.

The collar is gold and depicts Maltese Crosses, the ciphers SM and SG and crowned lions alternating.

Two winged lions each holding a book and seven arrows placed above a crown are at the collar's centre.

On "collar days" assigned by the Queen the members may wear the order's collar with a military uniform or morning wear.

The star of the order is worn on the left breast by the Knights and Dames Grand Cross and the Knights and Dames Commanders.

The star for the holders of the Grand Cross is comprised of Maltese Crosses seven armed and silver rayed. There is a gold section between each of these.

There is a red cross to denote St. George and the centre of the star is dark blue and shows the motto around an image of St. Michael slaying Satan.

The Knights and Dames Commander are permitted to wear a slightly smaller silver star, eight pointed with two Maltese Crosses. Again St. George and St. Michael appear and the motto is displayed.

The badge is worn on a blue and crimson ribbon by all classes of the order's recipients.

Knights and Dames Grand Cross wear it on a riband worn over the right shoulder to the left hip.

Knight Commanders and male Companions wear it around the neck, their female counterparts wear it attached to a bow on their left shoulder.

The badge is worn suspended from the collar on designated days.

Knights and Dames Grand Cross may surround their arms with a circlet bearing the order's motto and the collar.

Knights and Dames Commanders and Companions may show the circlet but not the collar around their arms.

The badge of the order should be shown hanging from the collar or the circlet as appropriate.

All of the collars issued since 1948 have been returned to the Central Chancery of the Orders of Knighthood.

Chapter 12 - Royal Victorian Order

About The Order

This award is personally bestowed by the monarch to people who have worked within the royal household or as ambassadors.

It was created in 1896 by Queen Victoria.

Since 1936 women and members of the Commonwealth have been eligible.

In Canada this honour is not used because the two highest grades would require a prefix to the recipient's name as their law stands.

There are several levels and post nominals

G.C.V.O. is for Knight or Dame Grand Cross

K.C.V.O. or D.C.V.O. is a Knight or Dame Commander

C.V.O. is a Commander

L.V.O. is a Lieutenant

M.V.O. is a Member

Since 1938 its spiritual home has been the Savoy Chapel in London, although the number of members has swelled so that the ceremonies held each four years have been relocated to St. George's Chapel at Windsor.

The monarch and the Knights and Dames Grand Cross are allotted stalls in the Savoy Chapel. Here, their stall plate, arms and the date that they joined the order are displayed.

Only the plate remains after the holder's death.

Its motto is "Victoria" and its appointed day is the 20th June.

The Grand Master of the order is H.R.H. Princess Anne, The Princess Royal.

Several members of British royalty hold the G.C.V.O., among them are the H.R.H the Duchess of Kent, H.R.H. the Countess of Wessex, H.R.H. Prince Michael of Kent and H.R.H. the

Duke of Gloucester.

Margaret Rhodes holds the L.V.O., she is a maternal cousin of

the Queen and a former lady in waiting to Queen Elizabeth,

the Queen Mother.

Deborah, Duchess of Devonshire was D.C.V.O., sadly she has

recently died. She received the order for her extensive work for

the Royal Collection Trust.

Robes and Insignia

Knights and Dames Grand Cross have a dark blue satin mantle that is edged in crimson satin. The lining is white satin.

There is a depiction of the order's star on the left.

They also have a collar which is comprised of alternating gold octagons showing a rose on a blue field and gold oblongs which have one of the following scripts inscribed in them:

Victoria Britt Reg.

Ind. Imp.

Def. Fid.

In English these mean Queen of the Britains', Empress of India and Defender of the Faith.

The octagonal medallion that hangs from the chain is blue, has red edging and shows a saltire and an image of Queen Victoria.

The medallion may also be used as a badge appendant.

The ribbon is red, white, red striped at the edges and blue in the central column for British recipients and the foreign members ribbon has an extra white stripe.

The width of the ribbon alters dependant on which rank of the order the person belongs to. Its narrowest width is 1.25 inches wide and for Knights or Dames Grand Cross it is 3.25 inches wide.

The badge is a Maltese Cross and the centre is a red medallion bearing the cipher of Queen Victoria. The blue border around the medallion bears the motto "Victoria" above a Tudor crown.

The Maltese Cross is in gold edged white enamel for Knights and Dames Grand Cross, Commanders and Lieutenants. All other recipients have a silver Maltese Cross.

The badge is sized according to the level within the honour. The largest is for the Knights and Dames Grand Cross.

The Knights and Dames Grand Cross and the Commanders have a star shape around their badge, for the Grand Cross it is an eight pointed silver star and for the Commanders it is a silver Maltese Cross with rays in silver lying between each arm of the cross.

The Knights and Dames Grand Cross wear it on a riband or sash from the right shoulder to their left hip. Knight Commanders wear it around the neck. Male Members, Lieutenants and Commanders wear the honour on the left breast.

The females in all of the levels below Dame Grand Cross wear their badge on a bowed ribbon on their left shoulder.

After death the Knights and Dames Grand Cross' collar must be returned although all other insignia may be retained by their descendants.

Chapter 13 - The Order of Merit

About The Order

It was created in 1902 by King Edward VII to recognise achievements in the armed forces, literature, art and science. Its motto is "For Merit."

The Order of Merit was first considered after the Battle of Trafalgar in 1805.

It was mentioned in correspondence between William Pitt, the Prime Minister and Lord Barham, the First Lord of the Admiralty.

The order was not created.

Queen Victoria, Prince Albert and several of her ministers wanted an award similar to the Prussian Pour le Merité to honour people who were not in public service.

Prince Albert met with the Prime Minister Robert Peel to

discuss the matter.

However, no Order of Merit was pursued until January 1888, twenty seven years after Prince Albert's death.

The Prime Minister Lord Salisbury drafted a constitution for the award.

He proposed that there would an Order of Merit in Science and Art but that it should be divided into two sections. The first was the "Order of Scientific Merit for Knights of Merit in Science" and the other was the "Order of Artistic Merit for Knights of Merit in Art."

The president of the Royal Academy, Sir Frederick Leighton, was against the proposed idea.

Again, the process stalled.

King Edward VII, Victoria's son, introduced the Order of Merit on 26th June 1902 without the divisions as shown above but with a military section.

The honour bore the distinction of being available to women from its creation.

Florence Nightingale was the woman first to accept it in 1907.

Interestingly, although Thomas Hardy, Sir Winston Churchill and J.M. Barrie accepted the order some high profile people did not including Rudyard Kipling and George Bernard Shaw.

Politicians tried to influence the King on who should receive the honour but it is a personal gift from the monarch. Private Secretaries suggestions were and are sought.

Between 1907 and 1913 portraits of the holders of the honour were painted by William Strang. The First World War ended this practice. The Queen revived the tradition in 1987 but each painting is produced by a different artist.

Prince Philip was given the Order of Merit in 1968 when he was forty seven years old. This makes him the youngest person to get the honour in its history.

Earl Mountbatten of Burma was the last holder of a military

Order of Merit.

The Order of Merit has a limit of twenty four people although this does not include honorary awards which the monarch may also bestow.

Today's members include the playwright Sir Tom Stoppard, naturalist and presenter, Sir David Attenborough, and the former Canadian Prime Minister Jean Chretien.

Nelson Mandela and Mother Teresa were both given the honorary versions of the order. There have been no honorary members since Mandela's death.

At the time of writing the twenty fourth place of the order is vacant.
The Queen is its sovereign and Lord Fellowes is the secretary and registrar for the order.

The letters O.M. may be used after the recipient's name.

In Britain the order does not give the holder any precedence over anyone else but in other Commonwealth realms it is positioned in different places in their order of precedence.

Insignia

There is an eight pointed badge showing a golden crown which has a red enamelled cross suspended from it, the centre of the cross is blue enamel.

A golden laurel wreath surrounds it and the motto "For Merit" is inscribed in gold letters.

The ribbon for the order is striped red and blue.

Men wear it around the neck and women have the ribbon tied in a bow on the left shoulder.

The military honour, should it ever be issued again, shows a pair of crossed swords in the centre.

The badges and ribbons must be returned upon the death of the holder. This instruction was enforced in 1991.

Chapter 14 – Imperial Service Order

About The Order

The Imperial Service Order was created in 1902 by King Edward VII.

There have been no new Imperial Service Order creations since government reforms in 1993 but the Imperial Service Medal is still issued to non managerial civil servants after twenty five years.

The Civil Service has many administrative and governmental roles.

The employees work in the public sector rather than the private sector.

Men and women were appointed to the Imperial Service Order when they retired after over twenty five years service.

It was given after sixteen years service if the location and conditions were exceptional.

There was no hierarchy within the order, all recipients were Companions.

The letters I.S.O. were placed after the recipient's name.

Insignia

The male holders of the order had an eight pointed star, the top point or ray had a crown over it.

At the centre of the star was a gold medallion with the monarch's cipher. The motto "For Faithful Service" surrounded the cipher.

The star was worn from a crimson red ribbon with a blue central stripe.

Ladies were given the same ribbon made in to a bow, the motto and the medallion but they had a silver laurel and a gold crown at the top.

Chapter 15 – The Most Excellent Order of the British Empire: G.B.E, K.B.E. and D.B.E.

King George V established the order on 4th June 1917, he wished to honour people who had worked, not necessarily fought, in the First World War.

Women were eligible for the honour from its creation.

St. Paul's Cathedral is the spiritual home of the order.

The motto is "For God And Empire."

A G.B.E, K.B.E or D.B.E. is awarded to a person who has made an outstanding and inspiring contribution to the nation.

Knight Grand Cross/Dame Grand Cross of the Most Excellent Order of the British Empire – G.B.E.

The Queen is the Sovereign of the Order and she appoints all of the members, normally after taking advice from the government.

Below her in rank is the Grand Master.

Prince Philip, the Duke of Edinburgh has held the position since 1953.

There have only been two other Grand Masters, Queen Mary between 1936 and 1953 and her son Prince Edward, Prince of Wales between 1917 and 1936.

Queen Mary was the first G.B.E., Dame Grand Cross in August 1917.

At any time there may be three hundred Knights and Dames Grand Cross.

Honorary Knighthoods are given by the Queen to people who are of a country where she is not the Head of State.

These knighthoods allow the person to use the post nominal letters but they are not addressed as Sir X.

Apart from Prince Philip the earliest appointed living Knights of the Grand Order are the British Sir Peter Le Cheminant and the Australian Sir Ronald Davison, they received the honour in 1978.

The most recent recipient at the time of writing is Sir John Bell, a Canadian.

Robes and Insignia

During ceremonial events the mantle worn by a Knight or Dame Grand Cross is purple satin lined with grey silk. Previously, it was made of yellow satin lined with blue silk.

The gold collar depicts the Royal Arms in six medallions, these alternate with six medallions showing the cipher of George V, GRI which stands for Georgius Rex Imperator. Gold chains or chains of lions and crowns connect the medallions.

On "Collar Days" the holder is permitted to wear military, formal or evening wear with their collar.

On less ceremonial occasions an eight pointed silver star is worn. Originally the ring showed an image of Britannia but King George V and Queen Mary's images have been used since 1937.

The badge is displayed on a sash or riband over the right

shoulder and the left hip.

It is an enamelled pale blue cross and crimson ring.

The circlet of the order with the badge suspended from it may be shown on the recipient's coat of arms.

The collars are returned to the crown after the death of its recipient.

Knight Commander or Dame Commander of the Most Excellent Order of the British Empire - K.B.E. or D.B.E.

The titles Knight Commander of the British Empire and Dame Commander of the British Empire were created in 1917 by King George V.

These rank below the G.B.E. in the Order of the British Empire.

There may be no more than eight hundred and forty five Knights and Dames Commanders at any time.

Dame Shirley Bassey is a D.B.E. and she received a C.B.E. in 1993.

Dame Judi Dench is a D.B.E. and a Companion of Honour, she received an O.B.E. in 1970.

Dame Maggie Smith is a D.B.E and a Companion of Honour, she received a C.B.E. in 1970.

Sir Jonathon Ive is a K.B.E. He is the Senior Vice President of

Design at Apple.

Insignia

The star of a Knight or Dame Commander is smaller than the one than a Knight or Dame of the Grand Cross (G.B.E.) may wear.

On less ceremonial occasions the eight pointed silver star is worn. Originally the centre showed an image of Britannia but King George V and Queen Mary's images have been used since 1937 surrounded by a red border.

The badge is enamelled with a pale blue cross patonce and a crimson border around the image of George V and Queen Mary, the border shows the motto.
A cross patonce is a cross that broadens, it is fleur-de-lis like at the end of each arm.

The badge is worn by males on a ribbon around the neck and ladies wear it from a bow on the left shoulder.

There is also a lapel pin for everyday wear.

The circlet of the order with the badge suspended from it may be shown on the recipient's coat of arms.

Notable Refusals

L. S. Lowry, the artist, declined a knighthood in 1968, a C.B.E. in 1961, and O.B.E. in 1955 and an appointment as a Companion Of Honour in 1972 and 1976.

He holds the record for the most honours declined by one person.

T.E. Lawrence or "Laurence of Arabia" declined a K.B.E. in 1918.

Alan Bennett, the playwright, declined the K.B.E. in 1996 and the C.B.E. in 1988.

Vanessa Redgrave refused the D.B.E. in 1999, she had accepted a C.B.E. in 1967.

Note: Knight Bachelor (K.T.) is not part of the Order of the British Empire.

It is given to people who are not in the peerage or in a senior position in the Order of Chivalry and it is the lowest form of knighthood although it has been in existence since Henry III's reign 1216-1272.

Michael Faraday, the acclaimed scientist, George and Robert Stephenson, the father and son railway engineers and inventors, Peter Benenson, the founder of Amnesty International and William Pember Reeves, a New Zealand politician are reputed to have declined the honour of Knight Bachelor.

Sir Ian McKellen holds the knighthood, the C.B.E. and he is a Companion of Honour.

Sir Patrick Stewart holds the knighthood and an O.B.E.

Sir Kenneth Branagh holds the knighthood.

Chapter 16 - The Most Excellent Order of the British Empire: C.B.E., M.B.E. and O.B.E.

The order was created by George V to honour people who had made valuable contributions in largely non-fighting roles throughout World War One.

Women were eligible for the honour from its creation.

St. Paul's Cathedral is the spiritual home of the order.
The motto attached to the order is "For God and the Empire."

Commander of the Order of the British Empire – C.B.E.

Commander of the British Empire is below a G.B.E., K.B.E. and D.B.E., it is given in recognition of a person's prominence at a national or regional level. It also celebrates innovation.

It was suggested by the House of Commons Select Committee in 2004 that the word Commander should be changed to Companion to make it sound less militaristic.

This has not happened.

There is a limit of eight thousand, nine hundred and sixty holders of this honour at any time.

Professor Stephen Hawking is a C.B.E. and a Companion of Honour.

Actress Catherine Zeta Jones is a C.B.E.

The comedian Barrie Humphries (Dame Edna Everage) is a C.B.E.

The writer Ruth Rendell is a C.B.E. and she holds a life peerage as Baroness Rendell of Babergh.

Insignia

The badge is worn by males on a ribbon around the neck and ladies wear it from a bow on the left shoulder.

It is a cross patonce, a red border with the motto inscribed surrounds George V and Queen Mary's image.

A lapel pin is available for everyday wear. These were introduced in 2006 for all holders of the Order of the British Empire.

The circlet of the order with the badge suspended from it may be shown on the recipient's coat of arms.

Notable Refusals

Actor Simon Russell Beale declined a C.B.E., he also declined K.T. in 2014.

Actress Honor Blackman declined a C.B.E. in 2002, she is not a monarchist and would prefer an elected leader.

J.G. Ballard, the writer, refused a C.B.E. in 2003 because he apparently did not like the honours system.

C.S. Lewis declined his C.B.E., he did not want to be associated with anything political.

Evelyn Waugh refused a C.B.E. in 1959 allegedly because he wanted a knighthood.

Officer of the Order of the British Empire – O.B.E.

The Officer of the British Empire award is given to people who make major contributions in an activity or area. These people would normally be known to the nation for their efforts.

It was suggested by the House of Commons Select Committee in 2004 that the name should be changed to Order of British Excellence to make it sound less militaristic. This did not happen.

There is no limit to the number of holders of O.B.E.'s but a maximum of eight hundred and fifty eight may be created in one year.

There are over one hundred thousand people alive who have received an O.B.E.

J.K. Rowling accepted her O.B.E. in 2000.
Novelist Ian Rankin received an O.B.E. in 2002.

Kylie Minogue received her O.B.E in 2008.

James Corden accepted his O.B.E. in 2015.

Insignia

The badge for Officers is a plain gold cross patonce.

A lapel pin is available for everyday wear. These were introduced in 2006 for all ranks in the order.

The O.B.E. is worn on a ribbon on the left breast by men and on a bowed ribbon on the left shoulder by women.

Notable Refusals

George Harrison of the Beatles is said to have felt that he should have been offered a knighthood like Sir Paul McCartney.

Roald Dahl declined an O.B.E., apparently he wanted a knighthood so that his wife could be titled Lady.

Nigella Lawson declined her O.B.E.

The poet Benjamin Zephaniah refused an O.B.E. in 2010 citing his hatred for the word Empire and what it means to him.

Member of the Order of the British Empire – M.B.E.

This honour recognises a significant achievement or outstanding service.

It is often awarded to people for beneficial local and community activities which set a positive and motivating example to others.

There is no limit to the number of Members but a maximum of one thousand four hundred and sixty four may be created in one year.

Actress Barbara Windsor received her M.B.E. in 2000.

Formula One driver Lewis Hamilton accepted a M.B.E. in 2009.

World number one golfer Rory McIlroy received his award in 2012.

Paralympian sprinter Jonny Peacock received his M.B.E. in 2013.

The entrepreneur and fashion commentator Caryn Franklin

also received her M.B.E. in 2013.

Insignia

The badge is a cross patonce of plain silver.

It is worn on the left breast by males and from a bow on the left shoulder by females.

A lapel pin is available for everyday wear.

Notable refusals

Joseph Corré, a co founder of Agent Provocateur is said to have refused his M.B.E. because he allegedly believed that the Prime Minister Tony Blair was "morally corrupt."

The Second World War hero Pearl Witherington was a Special Operations Executive (S.O.E.)
She refused the M.B.E. in 1945 because it was a civilian and not a military one.
She was offered and accepted a military M.B.E. in the same year.
She accepted a C.B.E. a number of years later.

.

Famous People Stripped of Their Honours

Although being stripped of an honour is a rare occurrence sadly it has happened.

The most usual reason appears to be a criminal conviction.

According to records an honour has been revoked one hundred and fourteen times to date, below are some of the famous people who have lost an honour.

Kim Philby was stripped of his O.B.E. in 1965. He had received the honour in 1946.

It had been discovered that he was a spy.

Lester Piggott, the champion jockey, was found guilty of tax fraud and his O.B.E. was revoked.

The entertainer Stuart Hall was stripped of his O.B.E. in 2013 after he was found guilty of indecent assault.

Another entertainer, Rolf Harris has been stripped of the C.B.E. that he received in 2006. He is serving a jail term of almost six years.

The boxing champion Prince Naseem Hamed was stripped of his M.B.E. in 2007 after he was jailed as a result of a car crash.

The darts player Phil Taylor had been nominated for an M.B.E. when he was convicted of indecent assault in May 2001. The M.B.E. was annulled.

In contrast, Sir Jeffrey Archer, the successful novelist and former politician did **not** lose his life peerage despite being found guilty of perverting the course of justice and perjury and serving time in prison from August 2001.

Chapter 17 - The Order of Companions of Honour

About The Order

Created by George V, it was first awarded on 4th June 1917.

It is sometimes considered as the Order of Merit's lesser order.

The Companion of Honour is given to someone who has made a major contribution in the fields of the arts, sciences, religion, industry or government.

Its motto is "In action faithful and in honour clear."

The order consists of the monarch and no more than sixty five Companions of Honour.

Honorary foreign members may be added to this number.

Originally the limit was fifty Companions of Honour but this was increased to sixty five in 1943 to allow:

Forty five from the United Kingdom.

Seven from Australia.

Two from New Zealand.

Two from South Africa.

Nine from India, Burma and the colonies.

In 1970 it was revised again:

Forty seven for the United Kingdom.

Seven for Australia.

Two for New Zealand.

Nine for other Commonwealth realms.

In 1975 New Zealand received an additional two places and the other Commonwealth realms number decreased to seven.

The monarch may take the advice from their governments on who should be given the honour.

Recipients of the order may use C.H. after their name. There is no precedence attached to the honour.

Politicians Menzies Campbell and Douglas Hurd, the actors Sir Ian McKellen, Dame Judi Dench, Dame Maggie Smith, athlete Dame Mary Peters and conductor Peter Maxwell Davies have been made Companions of Honour in recent years.

Insignia

Companions are issued with an oval medallion showing an oak tree, a shield with the Royal Arms of the United Kingdom hanging from a branch and to the left of the tree there is a knight in armour on horseback.

The badge's blue border has the motto inscribed on it in gold lettering.

"In action faithful and honour clear" was taken from Alexander Pope's work, Epistle to Mr. Addison.

The oval is surmounted by a crown.

Male members wear the badge on a red ribbon with golden border threads around their neck and females wear it on a bow on the left shoulder.

Notable Refusals

The poet and writer Robert Graves refused to be created a Companion of Honour in 1984, he had also declined a C.B.E. 1957.

As mentioned earlier, L.S. Lowry declined this honour among several others.

Conclusion

Centuries of history, influential and infamous characters have made the story of the British titles and honours so interesting to me.

There may always be detractors and those who believe that the titles and honours system have no place in a modern society but I'm proud and happy to say that I am not one of them.

Long may they continue.

I hope that you have enjoyed reading this book and learned a lot along the way.

Thank you

Joanne

You may be interested in my other books exclusive to Amazon including:

The British Royalty Quiz Book Series.

Royal Baby Names.

My website is at **www. joannehayle.co.uk**

My short stories are available on **www.alfiedog.com** and a selection of my children's stories have been published on **www.childrens-stories.net**

I also have a positive blog about O.C.D.,P.T.S.D. and my writing: _joannehayle.wordpress.com_